The IoT Product Manager

A Handbook for Engineers, Data Analysts, and Other IT Professionals

Padmaraj Nidagundi

Apress®

The IoT Product Manager: A Handbook for Engineers, Data Analysts, and Other IT Professionals

Padmaraj Nidagundi
Riga, Latvia

ISBN-13 (pbk): 978-1-4842-8630-2   ISBN-13 (electronic): 978-1-4842-8631-9
https://doi.org/10.1007/978-1-4842-8631-9

Managing Director, Apress Media LLC: Welmoed Spahr
Acquisitions Editor: Aaron Black
Development Editor: James Markham
Coordinating Editor: Jessica Vakili

Cover designed by eStudioCalamar

Cover image designed by Freepik (www.freepik.com)

Distributed to the book trade worldwide by Springer Science+Business Media New York, 1 New York Plaza, Suite 4600, New York, NY 10004-1562, USA. Phone 1-800-SPRINGER, fax (201) 348-4505, e-mail orders-ny@springer-sbm.com, or visit www.springeronline.com. Apress Media, LLC is a California LLC and the sole member (owner) is Springer Science + Business Media Finance Inc (SSBM Finance Inc). SSBM Finance Inc is a **Delaware** corporation.

For information on translations, please e-mail booktranslations@springernature.com; for reprint, paperback, or audio rights, please e-mail bookpermissions@springernature.com.

Apress titles may be purchased in bulk for academic, corporate, or promotional use. eBook versions and licenses are also available for most titles. For more information, reference our Print and eBook Bulk Sales web page at http://www.apress.com/bulk-sales.

Any source code or other supplementary material referenced by the author in this book is available to readers on GitHub (https://github.com/Apress). For more detailed information, please visit http://www.apress.com/source-code.

Printed on acid-free paper

Table of Contents

About the Author vii

About the Technical Reviewer ix

Acknowledgments xi

Introduction xiii

Chapter 1: History of Internet of Things 1

  1.1 IoT Making Our Cities and Homes Smart 4

  1.2 Becoming an Internet of Things Product Manager 7

    1.2.1 IoT Product Manager 8

    1.2.2 IoT Product Manager Duties and Responsibilities 10

  1.3 Steps to Become an Internet of Things Product Manager 12

    1.3.1 How to Become a Product Manager in IoT? 13

    1.3.2 What Skills Do You Need As a Product Manager with IoT? 14

  1.4 Why Companies Need an Internet of Things Product Manager 15

    1.4.1 Seven Reasons Any Company Hires Your Product Manager 16

    1.4.2 Internet of Things Product Manager Career Details
    and Qualifications 17

    1.4.3 Internet of Things Product Management Career
    Description and Salaries 17

    1.4.4 Internet of Things Product Manager Career Advice 18

Chapter 2: IoT Product Design 19

  2.1 Five-Step Process for IoT Product Design 21

  2.2 IoT Business Models 23

2.3 IoT Landscape 25

    2.3.1 IoT and Industry 4.0... 26

2.4 Three Types of Companies Working with IoT Today 27

2.5 IoT Hardware Components.. 33

2.6 Programming Platforms.. 37

Chapter 3: IoT Manager in the Agile Era...................................41

3.1 IoT Product Manager Journey.. 44

    3.1.1 Technology vs. Product... 46

    3.1.2 Team and People Management 46

3.2 First Four Months... 47

3.3 Role of IoT Manager in Organizations 50

3.4 IoT Product Manager Authority 54

    3.4.1 Defining Product Road Map for IoT....................................... 57

    3.4.2 Need Of Comprehensive Product Metrics and Quantitative Measurement Structure... 60

    3.4.3 Importance Of Implements Reporting Dashboards................ 63

    3.4.4 Partnering Closely with Key Stakeholders to Optimize Overall Product Adoption and Performance-Driven Growth 68

    3.4.5 IoT Manager End-to-End Development.................................. 74

Chapter 4: IoT Product Development and Life Cycle...........81

4.1 IoT Development Life Cycle.. 90

4.2 IoT Product Evaluation Metrics 94

4.3 Journey of an IoT Product... 98

Chapter 5: IoT Product Manager and Life Cycle Management.........109

5.1 IoT PM Conducts a Research 112

    5.1.1 IoT Development vs. Software Development.......................... 117

    5.1.2 IoT PM Focuses on Team Management 119

5.1.3 IoT PM Focuses on Product Strategic Decisions 124

5.1.4 IoT PM Focuses on Better Time Management Structures 127

5.2 Managing a Product Backlog 130

5.3 How an IoT PM Engages with Stakeholders to Scope Work......................134

5.4 How an IoT Product Manager Makes Critical Decisions............................136

5.5 How an IoT Product Manager Proposes Creative Solutions to Complex Problems 139

5.6 Four Steps to Launch and Operate a Secure IoT Product 143

Chapter 6: IoT Product Marketing **145**

6.1 What Makes a Good IoT Product 150

6.2 IoT Product Marketing Strategy 151

6.3 IoT Trends: Revenue and New IoT Business Models 154

Chapter 7: Government Regulation on IoT **161**

7.1 European Union (EU) Laws for IoT...161

7.2 United States (US) Laws for IoT 163

7.3 Canada Laws for IoT 166

7.4 Incorporate Standards and Regulations in Your IoT Product Strategy 167

7.5 IoT Product and Data Security 170

7.6 IoT Product Manager Skills for Future 174

7.7 IoT Products in 2030 176

Follow Along the Journey **179**

Suggestion for Future Work **185**

Index **189**

About the Author

 **Padmaraj Nidagundi** was born in 1985 in Vijayapura, Karnataka, India. He obtained his bachelor's degree in information science and engineering from Visvesvaraya Technological University (VTU). Master's degree in Computer Systems and Ph.D. in computer science from Riga Technical University. Since 2010, he has been working with different software development companies.

His most successful field of activity in previous years has been software development and testing, where he gained significant international work experience as an individual contributor, manager and leader. He is currently a researcher with Riga Technical University. In recent years, he has been a member of teaching staff and participated in many research projects. His research interests are software development, product management, smart cities, metaverse, quantum computing, cybersecurity, and artificial intelligence. He has a passion for innovation, solving complex problems.

About the Technical Reviewer

 **Sri Rajeth** is an innovative technology leader with 15 years of experience in software product management, project management, and technology consulting, as well as a track record of developing and launching technology products and solutions from concept to delivery. He's a result-oriented visionary with a unique background in IoT product development, software engineering, and design.

He is an expert in web and mobile applications, cloud infrastructure, Internet technologies, ecommerce, Fintech, EdTech, enterprise software, systems integration as well as experienced in owning programs in the digital transformation space – industrial IoT, IT/OT convergence, extended reality, blockchain, mobile apps and software frameworks, and digital payments. Over the years, he has built, led, and scaled high-performing teams of technologists at various organizations.

Acknowledgments

I would like to acknowledge the hard work of the Apress editorial team in putting this book together. I would also like to acknowledge the hard work of the Internet Society, Internet of Things Consortium, IoT Associations, Industry IoT Consortium, NASSCOM, and IoT Security Foundation for putting together products and communities that help to make the Internet of Things more accessible to the general public. Hurray for the democratization of technology!

Introduction

IoT now: IoT is the technology behind devices that are connected to the Internet. An IoT device can connect to other devices, collect data, and send it to a server for storage or analysis. These devices can be anything from wearables like fitness trackers, watches, or glasses; smart electrical outlets; thermostats; appliances; lights; robots – anything with an on-off switch!

As you may have guessed, there are many benefits of using IoT.

IoT future: Internet of Things is growing rapidly and transforming our world all around. It is a technology which will revolutionize to the extent that we can't even imagine. Internet of Things is connected with billions and billions of devices which are interconnected with each other to extend their capabilities by sharing information about numerous factors.

The future will be more intelligent where Internet-connected devices will connect to each other, in order to make our lives easier.

CHAPTER 1

History of Internet of Things

The Internet of Things (IoT) is the creation, implementation, and usage of connected devices that allow objects to exchange data via the Internet using wireless technologies. The intent behind developing IoT devices is to help increase productivity and convenience by enabling objects to provide information about themselves in order for humans, other machines, or business systems to operate more efficiently.

The term "Internet of Things" originally appeared in the year 2000. with the phrase "Internet of Things" coined by Kevin Ashton. Ashton was an Intel Fellow at the time, and he was working on a new platform that connected objects to the Internet. He aimed at providing more functionality to devices and introducing them to greater online interaction. His idea was revolutionary because it changed the way we interact with everyday objects. Connected objects are able to be sent data themselves and work autonomously as well (Figure 1-1).

© Padmaraj Nidagundi 2022
P. Nidagundi, *The IoT Product Manager*, https://doi.org/10.1007/978-1-4842-8631-9_1

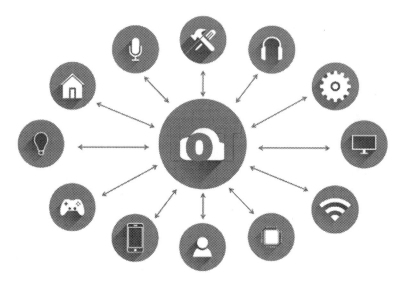

Figure 1-1. *IoT overview*

The term "IoT" was first coined by Tony Dyson, a British engineer, during a panel discussion at the BRITDOC Foundation Digital World conference in 1999. His concept was to connect the various things we use in our day-to-day lives and make them work more efficiently (Figure 1-1). In particular, he wished for people to be able to control their lights from remote locations and get reports of energy usage over the Internet. One of his initial suggestions was to create an Internet of Things where people receive information about things they own or use. This would make the product itself part of the Internet.

The idea was soon picked up by Ashton who had been working with Jacki Zehner, his then-girlfriend since 1995. After a minimal amount of research, he realized that object-centric technologies were a viable concept and that there really was no industry in place for them. Thus, they began to make plans to build such a system. Ashton first coined the term Internet of Things to describe their ideas because they believed that they would eventually have a sensor-equipped item at their home that could wirelessly exchange data with other connected devices.

While both Ashton and Zehner wished to introduce IoT into the marketplace, Ashton was focused on its business applications. In particular, he considered home automation as a suitable case for IoT technology because of its potential for bringing about productivity and convenience improvements in households. Home automation could also be a powerful tool to reduce energy consumption by having appliances switch on and off by themselves.

In the year 2010, IoT devices were first used in industry, particularly the automotive and transportation sector. However, the cost of making IoT devices still remained too high for the market to be able to use them widely. By 2014, however, the cost of IoT devices had come down significantly, thereby increasing their popularity and making them widely used across a wide variety of industries.

The use of IoT devices has increased significantly over the past few years primarily as a result of faster stabilization in technologies and software used with connected devices. These developments have improved IoT's economy and increased its prominence in the market.

The usage of IoT devices has increased significantly over the past few years primarily as a result of faster stabilization in technologies and software used with connected devices. These developments have improved IoT's economy and increased its prominence in the market.

IoT is currently expanding into industries such as healthcare, manufacturing, utilities, and transportation. By 2025, it is expected that there will be 250 billion connected devices just like smartphones we use in our daily lives today.

In the year 2026, the IoT market will have a compound annual growth rate of over 45%.

In recent years, the term IoT has been widely used to describe Internet-controlled machines, vehicles, and utilities. These items can be self-aware and are able to communicate with other devices. Many people have begun to think of IoT as a possibility for the future because it will allow people and machines to work in harmony to improve efficiencies or even save costs. The reason behind this is that IoT technology will allow humans and machines to function as one by allowing them to be connected automatically through the Internet.

Also, it is believed that by 2025, 40% of the world's population will be using Internet-enabled devices.

1.1 IoT Making Our Cities and Homes Smart

The Internet of Things is a big deal to many people, but why? What exactly does it mean? How is IoT making homes smart? This chapter will explain how IoT will make homes smarter, healthier, and more enjoyable for everyone.

In recent years, the Internet has transformed into many different platforms targeting the public. However, one of the biggest changes has been in technology's ability to act as a catalyst for rapid change and innovation.

It has long been said that technology has the power to change life in unimaginable ways. The Internet of Things (IoT) is one of those innovations that will alter our lives for the better.

In a recent article, *The New York Times* called the IoT "a giant game changer." For example, according to the article, "The Internet of Things means that we live in an increasingly connected world, but this new connectedness requires much more than just apps and widgets. It means taking a totally new approach to the way we design, build, and operate buildings, homes, and cities."

In other words, IoT is going to change how we live in buildings, homes, and cities. It will even change the way we think about our environment. This connectedness can do everything from make every building in a city smart to advise individuals on their lifestyles and wellness.

These IoT technologies are already being implemented all over the world. Here are some of the ways it's making homes smart.

1. It can be used to create a smart home environment. IoT can be used for a wide range of needs and purposes. For example, according to P&S Synergy Research Group, the global business spending on IoT technologies will reach $872 billion by 2027, up from $587 billion in 2022. These global IoT expenditures will support IoT adoption in a variety of ways.

Some ways include healthcare, transportation, environments and buildings, and more. It's easy to see how such a large investment in IoT can benefit the world.

For example, IoT can be used to monitor the environment. These sensors will collect data about temperatures, air quality, and more. These measurements will allow home occupants and building managers to know what's happening with the environment before confronting a problem. In addition, it'll also give property owners valuable information that they can use to make plans with their contractors or builders as well as run more efficient buildings.

Building managers will be able to get smart about every facet of their buildings. This knowledge can help them to provide better service and well-being to their customers. For instance, tenants will be able to monitor the building's energy consumption. They'll also be able to control whether the lights in the apartment go on or off on command, which helps make buildings more energy efficient.

2. It can prevent illness and disease through communication. Another way IoT will help to make homes smarter is through the Internet of Medical Things (IoMT). In other words, it will allow health professionals to monitor the health of their patients in new ways. For instance, IoMT can help people with diabetes take better care of their condition. In fact, it can help them keep up with their medication and be aware of life-threatening issues.

IoMT can even deliver medicine directly to patients' bodies when they need it most. In fact, IoMT can provide messages, pictures, and videos to patients who have linked their medical devices to their home networks.

They will also be able to send signals directly to the patient that help their bodies maintain good health; this is usually done through a smart pill bottle or other similar device.

3. It can provide suggestions for better lifestyle choices. There are many different ways that IoT will help people live healthier lives. For example, it can make recommendations on diet and exercise plans based on certain behaviors. It can also provide reminders to individuals based on their behavior and health status. For instance, IoT can remind individuals when to take their medication and how long it will wear off – for example, IoT could remind a person before a meal that they should take their allergy medicine.

In addition, IoT's ability to communicate with our bodies can help us maintain healthy lifestyles and lifestyles that are conducive to strong health. It can even deliver images and information to people when they need it most – like while they're sleeping.

4. It can be used to create a better, healthier workplace. These examples show that IoT can help make homes smarter by delivering the right information at the right time. However, the possibilities are endless when it comes to ways that IoT can help individuals live healthier lives. For instance, IoT can make workplaces more productive while improving employee satisfaction and well-being. According to Business Insider, smart systems and systems working together will eventually be able to track productivity by employees and adjust how they work based on their needs and schedules.

For example, IoT can remind an employee to take breaks when they need them. It can also help managers track the amount of breaks and lunches their employees take. Then, based on this new information, they can adjust schedules accordingly.

IoT can also help employers to know when all of the employees are at work and on break at any given time, which could improve productivity and lead to greater profits for their company.

5. It can be used to help improve security and safety. Smart buildings can also make other building systems more secure, too. For example, IoT can be used to allow building managers to monitor conditions in their buildings throughout the day or night. These conditions include whether doors are open or closed, whether alarms are sounding correctly, and so on. In addition, IoT can allow building managers to control the thermostats and other temperature controls in their buildings.

In fact, in the future, buildings will be able to recognize the identities of individuals who enter or leave the building. In turn, they'll be able to automatically adjust temperature and other settings based on the preferences of these individuals.

6. It's a key component in allowing smart cities to exist. For example, IoT can be used to create "smart" cities where there are lower energy consumption and less traffic congestion but improved productivity and better quality of life. According to a report by the McKinsey Global Institute, some cities around the world that are already on their way toward making this type of smart city transformation include Milan, China; Oklahoma City; and Austin.

McKinsey believes that intelligent buildings in these cities could save governments and private businesses billions of dollars every year through data analysis. For instance, intelligent buildings will be able to reduce energy consumption in these cities by 10% or more.

1.2 Becoming an Internet of Things Product Manager

The Internet of Things (IoT) is a space where technology and human ingenuity meet to create new and exciting opportunities. IoT products and services are capable of delivering meaningful insights about the world we live in while also facilitating more efficient interactions with everyday objects.

Product managers are under pressure to produce successful products that satisfy the needs of the customer while making a profit for their company. But with technology changing so quickly, it's hard for them to know where they should put their focus.

The Internet of Things is driving innovation in many sectors, but few industries have felt its impact more than product management. The popularity of IoT products has risen rapidly, and with them all the different ways in which they can be used. As product managers, we are tasked with producing successful products that satisfy the needs of our consumers while making a profit for our company. But companies and business find it challenging to determine where to focus because technology is evolving so quickly.

IoT is creating new opportunities for companies in unexpected places. Companies who have so far focused on physical products are adding the virtual components needed to connect these products to the Internet. They are using this online connection to improve the services associated with their product or to make products that we never knew were possible. Companies who have focused on digital products are adding Internet connectivity and sensors to their software, enabling them to connect in ways that we never thought was possible.

I wrote this chapter to help product managers understand how they can be better prepared for this fast-changing marketplace and provide insights into how IoT can be used in order to please all stakeholders.

Understanding its potential, this chapter will provide an overview of what it is like to become a product manager in the IoT space. It will also detail the skills, duties, and responsibilities required to excel in this growing field.

1.2.1 IoT Product Manager

It is important for a product manager to have both technical knowledge and business acumen. This combination of skills allows the IoT product manager to bridge the gaps between functional teams and ensure that the technology meets business requirements. That being said, some companies may look for a more general product management professional with technical skills on top of their core responsibilities.

It's important to note that the IoT product manager will most likely be involved in multiple domains (i.e., technical, business) on a daily basis (Figure 1-2). They work closely with product managers and engineers to ensure that their products are ready for the market and that they are also implementing a strategy that can live beyond the initial launch. That being said, they may also be more involved in business-related issues, like forecasting or negotiating deals with partners.

Figure 1-2. *IoT product manager duties and responsibilities*

As an IoT product manager, you will be responsible for a broad range of activities that might seem foreign to product managers who have been in the space for a while. You will need to be able to work across multiple teams in order to achieve your goals and support your organization's vision and mission.

1.2.2 IoT Product Manager Duties and Responsibilities

1. **Build a product**: When you're in a new company, you will be responsible for building the initial product and defining its features. This can include working with your engineering team to build out an MVP (minimum viable product) on top of an existing platform. If you're in a very early stage startup, it might be necessary to start from scratch, but this will require more research and insight into your industry.

2. **Analyze data**: This refers to gathering and analyzing the initial product's user feedback. You will also be involved in defining what the product should look like, as well as how it should function within the world (i.e., how it will work on a smartphone). This includes implementing features that you know the market wants in the short term, but may not make sense for a planned long-term strategy.

3. **Build a strategy**: After the initial analysis, you will be responsible for building the product road map, giving updates to the board of directors and marketing teams about what is coming and when. You will take an active role in ensuring your

stakeholders are aware of new developments, but that it's okay to have a slow or staggered launch when required. This will also include coordinating with other departments on how best to communicate these changes with the end users.

4. **Market the product**: The final responsibility of an IoT product manager is to market the product to a wider audience and drive awareness around it. You will ensure your team manages all aspects of the marketing process, like obtaining testing with beta testers and conducting live events. You can also work with the sales team to drive business development efforts that can help achieve short-term revenue targets as you build your team.

5. **Lead a team**: The IoT product manager will be responsible for leading a team of experts who have specific knowledge and experience in their respective fields. You will ensure there are clear lines of communication between all teams, as well as ensuring that everyone is aware of the latest news and updates. This includes attending weekly or biweekly meetings to discuss progress on the product and strategize for upcoming features.

6. **Oversee operations**: Finally, the IoT product manager is responsible for overseeing the operation of the product after launch. This includes performing customer research and testing to ensure the product meets user needs and that it's easy to use in real-world situations. This can include educating users about how to use your product

as well as modifying a new feature according to customer feedback. You will also be responsible for ensuring that support teams are trained on how to assist customers with any problems they may encounter while using your product.

1.3 Steps to Become an Internet of Things Product Manager

The Internet of Things (IoT) is a huge market opportunity and one that many people are getting excited about. A rapidly growing number of devices connect to the Internet, giving us the opportunity to automate processes, manage data, and reduce our environmental footprint. However, working with this technology can be complex, and drawing from existing product management skills is not enough. It requires an understanding of the IoT environment and how to develop the right product for this market.

The word "product" has different meanings in the digital world. Depending on which industry you're in, product managers can be responsible for creating different kinds of products. In the case of the Internet of Things, it is a product that brings together hardware and software to create a new market. These devices and software run on platforms that enable devices to collect data from real-world environments such as factories or homes.

The product manager plays many roles within a product team. Firstly, they must be able to define and communicate requirements, ensure that concepts and ideas are developed through to a concept model, select and manage suitable technologies, then build the product to specification, lastly, testing prototype in customer environment until product is fully fit for production. Product managers are now being asked more about their technical capabilities as IoT becomes more forefront in what we do as a business.

To become a product manager in the IoT area, you need to have experience working in technology. However, there are not always any positions available; you need to work across different departments and gain the skills required by product managers. You can work across numerous areas of the business such as strategy, operations, sales, or marketing. It's also useful to have an understanding of the principles behind technology development.

You may also need to bid for different types of projects such as product definition, concept development, and prototype. Understanding your position within the organization and where you fit into the product life cycle will give you the best chance of gaining experience. For example, if you're selected for a role in concept development, then you must be able to work within a close team of project managers and designers to develop products that are appropriate for customers and technology partners.

How can you get experience in IoT? You can either find a role at a startup or become an intern at an organization that uses IoT technology. For example, Siemens has created a software development programmer called "the Program for Internet of Things."

1.3.1 How to Become a Product Manager in IoT?

- Work in different departments and gain experience with technology.

- Create your own product ideas and pitch to the relevant department.

- Take part in local events and join communities to meet peers and share knowledge.

- Understand your role within the life cycle you can bid for projects that are right for you. For example, work on concept development is best suited to someone who can work with prototypes within an agile environment.

13

- Learn the IoT business and technologies by reading chapters, attending events, and studying relevant papers.

- Build a portfolio of work highlighting your knowledge and experience in the IoT environment. A good example would be a visual presentation of your understanding of IoT value chain.

- Publish your own chapters or videos to promote your ideas to peers and other people in the IoT industry. This will show you have an interest in this area and have thought about how you can make products better.

- Learning about hardware and software used in an IoT project make you better in product management. Get information about the company and how it functions. This would include the products and services they offer and how they work with other businesses.

1.3.2 What Skills Do You Need As a Product Manager with IoT?

- Experiences in the technology domain and you must have technical understanding of hardware and software used in IoT projects. Be able to communicate with relevant technical people to get this information.

- Identification of new/existing customer/business and you must be able to communicate your product ideas to different departments within a company.

- You must be able to work both in product management and within a technical environment. This means being able to set up test environments and manage data related to the IoT project. Also knowledge of wireless core networks, such as HLR/HSS, PGW, PCRF/OCS, MME, SGW, SMSC, VoLTE, SMS over IP, 5G, IoT Cloud computing platforms (Azure / AWS / IBM / Google ..etc) is preferred. You need to identify client needs and help team members, communicate with sales representatives, and customer facing meetings as the subject matter expert.

- You must be able to write documentation and explain how to use the product and create compelling experience strategies in collaboration with UX. Finally create and put into action a thorough product marketing plan.

1.4 Why Companies Need an Internet of Things Product Manager

The Internet of Things (IoT) is a network of devices and sensors embedded in everyday objects and environments. These devices collect data and provide real-time information, so that the intelligence gathered can be used to manage and monitor systems. The IoT generates large amounts of data which is too much for people to consume or analyze on their own, so it's important to have specialists on staff – especially if you are an organization looking to get ahead in this new era.

1.4.1 Seven Reasons Any Company Hires Your Product Manager

- You have a thorough understanding of the product and business requirements.

- You are able to guide other people in the team who do not have this expertise.

- You can respond to inquiries of customers on the status of their orders, support requests, and changes to service plans by means of written and/or verbal communications.

- You are able to manage teams who either do not have the same expertise as you or are unable to independently manage a product, in order to translate requirements into products.

- You can help companies advance the state of technology and adopt technologies for which there is not yet consumer demand.

- You have a thorough understanding of the product and business requirements, so that you can advise management on strategy and product development plans, as well as make sure that your team delivers on those plans.

In this section, we'll explore the world of Internet of Things product management and showcase how you can make an impact on your organization. We'll look at what it takes to become a successful IoT product manager from both a personal and professional perspective.

1.4.2 Internet of Things Product Manager Career Details and Qualifications

There are two main tracks for being an IoT product manager: hardware and software. Software products have a more complex development cycle than hardware, so they require more time to develop and test. So if you are looking for a career in the software field, Employers hiring for! A relevant degree person, such as a Bachelor's or Master's in Computer Science, Engineering, MBA, Business, Electronics and communication, or IoT product development education, is typically preferred by employers when hiring for the product manager IoT position.

Also, some of the following titles might be a little outdated, so check out the latest ones listed on Indeed.com to find out more about new trending positions.

1.4.3 Internet of Things Product Management Career Description and Salaries

An IoT product manager is responsible for determining enterprise requirements and creating a technical road map. They are responsible for developing their organization's vision with regard to the IoT and ensuring that it's achieved. They work closely with companies in order to integrate the product into their systems and ensure that it is up to date and as required.

Today, these roles, career job description can get quite complex as you move from small devices to mainstream products. For example, a data analytics IoT product manager faces different challenges than a LED bulb product manager. A data analytics product manager might have to deal with the discovery of various costs and redundant usage of data across various departments in the company. You can find data analytics IoT product managers earning $100,000 and up.

Due to the complexity of IoT products and the new technologies involved, software product managers also earn a good salary. If you are looking for an entry salary for this field, check out Indeed.com's top salary for software product managers (with over 100 job postings) at $119,000 or higher when compared to other IT jobs.

1.4.4 Internet of Things Product Manager Career Advice

The best advice that I have is to do whatever you enjoy and love to do. The Internet of Things industry is changing so fast, it's hard to keep up with the trends, but it doesn't mean you can't do your best and focus on bringing your ideas to life.

Also, make sure you surround yourself with people who are smarter than you. This will help you improve your skills and learn new things every day.

IoT product manager advice: "Despite the fact that this is an emerging technology, there are many companies involved in its development. I think it's good to have a network of people who have created real-world products using IoT platforms and can provide you with invaluable advice."

—Martin Musatov,
Chief Technical Officer of GreenPeak Technologies

CHAPTER 2

IoT Product Design

The product design of IoT is a huge topic and will become even more so with the age of devices like the "egg" and the "vest." The interconnectedness between these various pieces, and how they connect to our brains, is difficult to fathom. But what we can do is understand the UI and UX in their simplest forms in order to begin understanding this new type of design (Figure 2-1).

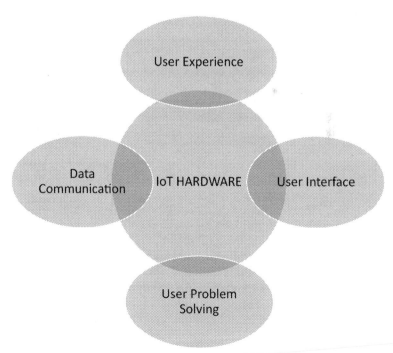

Figure 2-1. *IoT and user interface connection*

© Padmaraj Nidagundi 2022
P. Nidagundi, *The IoT Product Manager*, https://doi.org/10.1007/978-1-4842-8631-9_2

There are four key elements when designing an IoT product: the device itself, the communication technology, the user interface, and the interface between all of these.

There are four main components to the product design of an IoT device or system: devices, data communication, user interface, and web/mobile interfaces (especially interactive UIs).

The first thing we need to understand is that an IoT device can be connected to many different types of networks and ecosystems. There are cellular networks, satellite networks, NFC, Bluetooth, and, of course, the Internet. The first three are only used when the device is not connected to the Internet. They have their own user interface elements specific to each technology, but they all have one thing in common: It doesn't matter what part of the world the product is in or who the operator of that network is; you still use its basic functions. These technologies are not decentralized by design; they are all centralized resources.

What you absolutely cannot do with an IoT device is decentralize the network. In other words, you cannot rely on a third party or another network to make sure that the data it is transmitting won't be intercepted. That would make the device completely untrustworthy and useless for real-world applications. It would not be able to perform its primary function.

The first generation of IoT devices were all centralized. All devices were connected to a central database. The next generation of devices will always be centralized. That is because becoming decentralized would require the amount of processing power necessary for real-time interaction and interaction on the scale required for IoT applications.

As we start to push the limits of what operation a device can do, it becomes important to "decentralize" it.

2.1 Five-Step Process for IoT Product Design

A five-step process to define the best user experience for all users across the IoT technology stack (Figure 2-2).

Step 1: Identify the Most Important Function of Your IoT Service

The first thing to figure out is what your service actually does. Ask yourself, what would happen if I were to turn it off? Will my life be different if that happens? If the answer is yes, then we will want to design the user interface and UX directly for people who need this function. If it's no, then we are fine with designing the UX for everyone. We will allow people to live without the service as long as they are not inconvenienced by it.

Step 2: Determine the Ideal Users of Your IoT Service

We also have to find out what type of user is ideal for this IoT product. What we want is an end user who understands how to use it, why they need it, how it works, and how to operate it. They will interact with the system and make decisions about what the data means for their lives. The ideal user is also the person who will invite people to use the product if they do not already have it.

Step 3: Define a User Experience Design

Once you have identified the most important function of your IoT service, you need to determine what user experience is best for that function. The choice of UX may sound simple, but it's actually more complex than it looks. The choice has everything to do with where the service is used and how many people are likely to interact with it. If you choose an experience that is not appropriate for your service or company, then it will be a completely wasted investment and not the best use of resources.

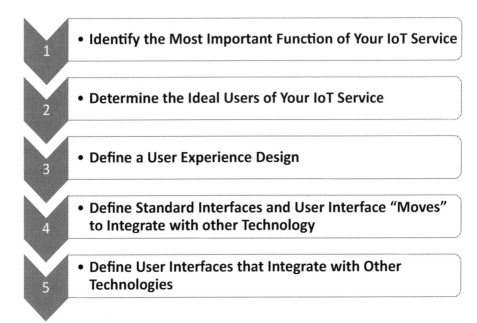

Figure 2-2. *A five-step process for IoT product design*

Step 4: Define Standard Interfaces and User Interface "Moves" to Integrate with Other Technologies

We also need to define the overall user interface design of the product and standard ways of interacting with other products. For example, it may be important for you to integrate with another product. You need to decide what is the best way for a user to pick up the product and interface with it.

Step 5: Define User Interfaces That Integrate with Other Technologies

The last thing we have to do is define an interface that allows other devices and systems to connect and integrate with the product through their own experience of using it. This means defining how your individual device will communicate with other devices in real time.

There is so much to consider when designing an IoT product, but these five steps can take you a long way to developing the perfect solution.

Now, let's explore a little bit more about each step of this process. The first step is identifying the most important function of your IoT service. Ask yourself, what would happen if I were to turn it off? Will my life be different if that happens? If the answer is yes, then we will want to design the user interface and UX directly for people who need this function. If it's no, then we are fine with designing the UX for everyone. We will allow people to live without the service as long as they are not inconvenienced by it.

2.2 IoT Business Models

Many projects have failed because they have been trying to sell the product rather than the service. It's too easy to say "our product is X" and miss out the real opportunity. A product manager needs to understand what main business opportunities can be delivered. The IoT has multiple business models (Figure 2-3) to consider as well as new technologies that can deliver different services, for example:

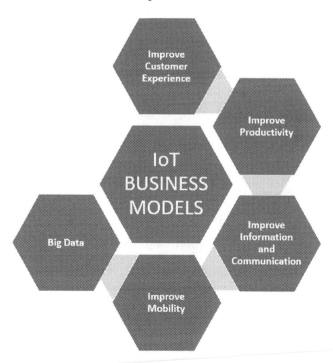

Figure 2-3. *IoT business model*

Improve customer experience: The focus is on how it improves a person's experience (e.g., banking apps, online shopping platforms).

Improve productivity: This will focus on automating processes and improving productivity.

Improve information and communication: A business could offer services that help businesses communicate with each other, for example, a device that monitors stock in the event of a supplier not being available.

Improve mobility: People expect to receive information no matter where they are, as in emerging markets many people have mobile phones but no postal contacts.

Big data: Many IoT services are being driven by customer data, such as monitoring traffic on a road or providing information about the weather.

The question is, how do we create new value? How do we make the old value better?

We must think about our business from the customer's point of view.

For example, buying a smartphone would be like buying your own personal assistant. It should give you useful information on your running and cycling habits and help you to find a restaurant with good reviews; it should have access to all your contacts and calendar. In these ways, it will impact many aspects of your life; therefore, it will prove extremely valuable to you.

Customer experience is all about the connection between the customer and the outcome of the IoT. This means that there are many different ways to monetize the value. If a company isn't in a position where it can fully benefit from that value, then they aren't really in a position to sell it.

For example, if you were to sell your data as personalized advertising, you wouldn't be able to use it for much else. This is why it's important to present how the data can be used in a cost-effective way. For example, if you have a car with GPS tracking, then you can share the data with local shops and make money back by getting discounts when you come into the store. This is more likely to happen because it's of value to both parties.

The rules are changing, and we're moving from vertical silos (e.g., automotive companies making their own components) to horizontal silos (e.g., car-sharing companies). This will change the way IoT is being used. This is because there is a need to reach out to customers outside of the company itself.

For example, car-sharing companies can use their platform as a customer service for passengers by providing information about nearby parking spaces, street parking, and public transportation. The car-sharing company will also be able to sell access to drivers for other services it offers, such as recommending restaurants nearby or marketing targeted information about services and events.

IoT can be used for monitoring people in other ways. There is a risk of privacy issues, and so there is a need to be transparent about the value of the information being collected. It's all about putting the customer in control.

As an example, if we know how often you go to restaurants, then we will be able to recommend restaurants that would suit your profile. This could also help people with allergies, for example, by recommending restaurants with nut-free food or soy milk for your coffee.

This example could also be used for hotel booking through a partner network.

2.3 IoT Landscape

As we all know, the Internet of Things (IoT) is a network of physical objects, such as retail merchandise and machines, connected to the Internet and to each other.

Before we dive into this chapter in detail and explore IoT's ongoing development in context with social, economic, and technological advancements, we feel it is important to reflect on what this movement means for our well-being.

The IoT landscape is booming, and it is being embraced by giants such as IBM, Google, and Microsoft. The IoT has already transformed the way we live and work. As a result, the IoT industry is expanding (Figure 2-4).

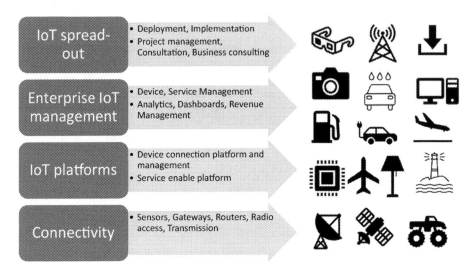

Figure 2-4. *Modern IoT landscape*

2.3.1 IoT and Industry 4.0

As smart homes become a reality, the IoT will impact every aspect of our lives – from home security to lighting control systems in our workplaces/homes and to automated drone delivery of goods. The Internet of Things anticipates a world where "everything is connected." IBM predicts that by 2025, the IoT will generate more than $9 trillion in economic value. This is disrupting entire industries and sectors as we know them today.

What does this mean for your company? As consumers, we are becoming more demanding than ever with our expectations from brands and the experiences they offer us. The consumer's role has now evolved into a "customer author," meaning that consumers are actively involved in product design, development, and marketing (i.e., crowdfunding).

As customers, we are looking for emotional value from brands. We are increasingly demanding transparency and more personalized experiences from brands. These new customer preferences will drive innovations in the service sector as well as stimulate growth for a variety of industries such as insurance, retail, and finance.

The IoT will influence our future in ways we can't yet imagine. It is estimated that by 2025, there will be a whopping 6 billion connected devices and sensors surrounding us each day.

2.4 Three Types of Companies Working with IoT Today

As shown in Figure 2-5, the current IoT landscape can be identified by three types of companies.

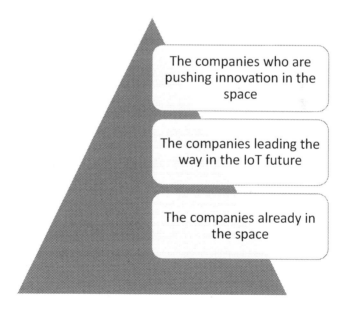

Figure 2-5. *Main types of companies in the IoT field*

In recent years, the Internet of Things (IoT) has been a rapidly growing field with increasing complexity. To cut through the noise, we've got a top five list of technologies and categories including big companies that have made their bones in the IoT and where you should expect to see them over time. We've also included a section on the technologies some smaller companies are currently working on.

1)   The companies already in the space

1. Alphabet (Google)

Alphabet was the first company to develop light bulbs, which means they were also the first to develop smart light bulbs. They've already been toying around with Nest, which is an IoT company that focuses primarily on home automation, and now they've also released Google Home and Amazon Echo competitors. Clearly, it looks like home automation is of high interest for Alphabet.

2. Cisco

Cisco has been in the IoT game since the beginning, so it's no surprise to see them leading the way in this category. They're a company that's really pushing a lot of what they've learned and developed on networking, so expect to be seeing a lot more home security and home automation products from them in the future.

3. IBM

IBM has spent decades mastering enterprise technology and has had some success with their Watson Intelligent Assistant. In the IoT category, IBM is focusing on their new Bluemix cloud and their Watson IoT Platform to help businesses develop, manage, and monitor sensors.

4. Intel

Intel has been a longtime player in the PC market and has even served as a sponsor for some of the greatest PC games ever made. They're now interested in developing technologies that can sync up your PCs, VR gear, and other devices to make them all work together more efficiently.

5. Microsoft

Microsoft has probably spent more time than any other company developing their product suite for the home market. They've got a bit of a reputation in the space, and most people are anxiously waiting to see how Microsoft will be innovating in the space over time.

6. Samsung

Samsung is not a company you typically associate with smart homes and IoT, but they're definitely interested in that space and have already been working on it for quite a while. Their acquisition of SmartThings shows that they are serious about making sure they're the ones changing the game in this category.

7. Sony

Sony isn't a company you typically associate with the IoT, but then again, Sony is not a company you typically associate with producing video games for PCs either. They've got quite a history of being innovative in the tech space, and if you look carefully, you'll see that they have been experimenting with AI and IoT for quite some time now.

8. Google-owned Nest

Nest, who is owned by Alphabet (Google), has been around for as long as you can remember, and they're one of the most innovative and popular home automation technologies available today. They've got quite a bit of greenhouses in their future, and they've already been experimenting with connected cars, so expect to be seeing a lot more from them over time.

2)   The companies leading the way in the IoT future

1. Samsung

Samsung has been experimenting with smartwatches for a long time now and seems to be incredibly interested with not only developing electronics but also developing an ecosystem that will be able to work seamlessly together. Their acquisition of Vivint, a smart home tech company, shows they're serious about making sure they're adding to the IoT ecosystem.

2. Google

Google is clearly the leader of the pack when it comes to so-called "smart" companies. They've had experience in the business world for as long as anyone can remember and have been working on AI algorithms for years. It's also no surprise to see that they're focusing heavily on the home automation market and they're holding an event soon where they'll be talking more about their IoT plans.

3. Apple

Apple has already been experimenting with smartwatches, but it looks like they're now ready to move into the smart home arena by purchasing HomeKit developer ApplesByte. This acquisition means Apple is definitely going to be focusing on the home automation space and developing products that will work together with other Apple devices.

4. Amazon

Amazon has been working on smart speakers for some time now, but they've got a long way to go before they can even come close to competing with Google. They've still got a long way to go in terms of smart home technology, and we're sure they'll continue to hold their own as a major player in this space.

5. IBM

IBM has been working on a lot of AI technologies over the years, and if you look into their history, you'll see that they've been developing AI algorithms for quite some time. They've also partnered with some manufacturers to be able to use AI to analyze and understand how people interact with smart devices.

6. Apple-owned Beats Electronics

Apple bought Beats specifically so they could work together with Dr. Dre and help him develop an ecosystem of audio products that work together. They're both working on a wireless headphone ecosystem with the goal of making it easy for people to seamlessly move between different electronics in their lives.

7. Google-owned Nest

Nest was purchased by Alphabet (Google) a while ago, so they've already been involved with some smart home technology. They're pushing forward with their Nest Protect and learning an awful lot about home automation, which is going to make them much more valuable as time goes on.

8. Microsoft-owned Skype

Skype has been around for a while now, but they've only recently developed a way to work with objects and other devices in your home. They're also working on more advanced AI algorithms, and we're sure they'll continue to be innovating in this space as well.

9. Sony-owned Sony Smart Audio Technology

Sony owns the audio company Sony Smart Audio Technology, and it looks like they're developing speakers that will work together with other AI-powered technologies. They're targeting a variety of different types of sounds and creating an ecosystem that will allow people to better navigate their home sound system.

3) The companies that are pushing innovation in the space

1. Google

Google is always interested in improving their search technology, and they're looking at ways to make it easier for people to use voice technology in order to do some simple tasks around the house. They've even put out some videos showcasing how you might be interacting with your home tech soon and it looks interesting.

2. Intel

Intel is one of the biggest players in the tech industry, and they're working with Advantech to push forward in terms of their home automation technology. They're also currently running a competition challenging people to become the next generation of IoT developers.

3. GE Digital

GE Digital has been working on home automation technology for some time now, and they've also been heavily focused on using data collection technology to make sure people can be more efficient at home. They've put out a number of devices that help people to better manage their energy, and that's an impressive display of innovation.

4. Google-owned Nest

Google has been working on home automation for a long time now, and they're using AI to develop connected devices that are able to work together with voice technology. They're also interested in making sure they can collect data from smart devices, which will allow them to be more efficient at what they do.

5. Microsoft-owned Skype

Microsoft has been putting out a lot of products that are hardware independent, meaning they're software and hardware agnostic, which will allow them to fit in well with any connected environment. They've also developed their own IoT platform called WireLur, which is currently in open beta testing.

6. Samsung

Samsung has been working on home automation technology for a while now, and they've got some highly effective products on the market. They've also developed Tizen, a new operating system that's going to make it easier for people to operate their electronics.

7. Xiaomi

Xiaomi is a Chinese company that's working on home automation technology, and they're trying to develop affordable devices that will be able to do some pretty cool things. They've been able to create devices that are not only easy to use but are extremely affordable as well.

8. Lenovo

Lenovo has been working on AI smart home technology for a while now, and they're putting out some impressive devices that are compatible with other devices in your home. They've got a couple of products being released this year, but they're keeping quiet about what exactly they'll be releasing.

9. Google-owned Nest

Nest recently put out a new product called the Nest Hello, which is a new type of security system that works alongside Google Assistant to help people to get better at their home automation technology. They've also developed a voice-activated learning thermostat, which is going to be useful to people that are trying to automate the temperature in their home.

There are so many great companies working on home automation technology right now, and there's still plenty of innovation ahead of us. We can't wait to see what these engineers come up with as we continue toward the future of smart homes.

2.5 IoT Hardware Components

As shown in Figure 2-6, the five main IoT hardware components are

- Sensors

- Wireless module

- Microprocessor

- Microcontroller

- Memory

The sensors are used to detect changes in the environment or other sensors. They also collect data related to the world around them. A wireless module is needed for communications between the device and an outside network (such as Wi-Fi, Bluetooth, etc.). A microprocessor is responsible for executing instructions stored in memory. A microcontroller is a small computer on a single integrated circuit that uses a microprocessor to control and monitor devices such as sensors. It is not necessary to know the internal structure of each of these components.

Some examples of sensors are optical, seismic, proximity, temperature, humidity, pressure sensors, and others. The data from these devices is transmitted to the IoT gateway through wired or wireless networks. From gateway, it will be transmitted to the cloud platform for storage and analysis.

There are several types of wireless networks globally. The basic difference is based on the types and characteristics of the communication protocols used. Each type has its own advantages and disadvantages. Some wireless technologies are more prone to interference, some have faster transmission rate, but some require less power, etc. In this chapter, we will only mention the most widespread wired networks for communications between IoT devices and gateway and cloud platforms:

- RS-232, RS-485

- Wi-Fi (802.11b, 802.11g, and 802.11n)

- Bluetooth V2.1+EDR

- Zigbee (2.4 GHz, 868 MHz) and Zigbee (902 MHz)

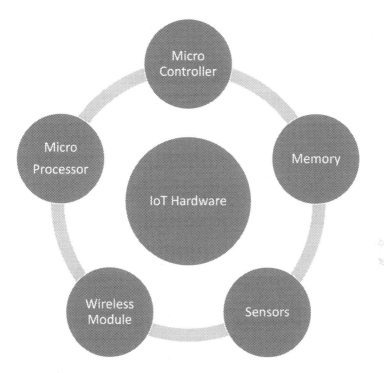

Figure 2-6. *Overview of IoT main hardware components*

There are two types of cloud platforms: private and public or hybrid (private or public). The private cloud is managed by a single organization and is not open to any third party, while the public cloud is managed by a third-party organization and is open for all customers. The hybrid cloud combines both types of cloud platforms.

IoT devices are connected to the cloud platform via a secure and reliable communications mechanism. The cloud platform provides a balance between cost, performance, stability, and ease of use. Some common characteristics of the most successful IoT platforms are

1. Multithreaded architecture

2. High-performance gateway with 10/100/1000 Mb Ethernet ports

3. Efficient hardware and software architecture

4. Strong cryptography, encryption algorithms, protecting the data from interference from other devices and unauthorized users

5. Various communication protocols for wireless networks: WiMAX, Wi-Fi, Bluetooth V2.1+EDR, Zigbee, and others

6. High reliability of the communication channel(s) between IoT devices and the cloud platform

7. Low latency and high responsiveness of the cloud platform

8. High reliability of the communication protocol(s)/ protocol stack(s) between IoT devices and the cloud platform

9. Open architecture, flexibility (modularity, scalability) and ease of use, good documentation

The main advantages of an IoT platform are the increase in productivity, introducing new business opportunities, and improvements in security. The IoT is a powerful tool for smart cities, digital health, connected factories, or smart homes. There are several possible applications of the IoT:

- Remote monitoring, control, and management

- Remote or local power grid, metering, and pricing

- Remote or local energy storage (electricity and energy usage)

- Remote or local electricity generation, transmission, and distribution

- Implementation of introduction of smart purchasing

- Implementation of introduction of a smart retail environment (to reduce operational costs, increase profit)

- Digital health (storing data on patients' health condition for better diagnosis and treatment)

- Digital education (improving teaching process; from this perspective, the role of the cloud platform is essential)

2.6 Programming Platforms

There are many IoT programming platforms; the top five platforms are

1. Google Cloud IoT Platform

2. IBM Bluemix

3. Microsoft Azure IoT

4. Amazon Web Services Platform for IoT

5. IBM Watson IoT Platform

The following are some of the factors used for selecting the platform: cost, scalability, security, flexibility, and ease of use. The most cost-effective platform for such projects is Google Cloud IoT Platform, whereas the most scalable one is Microsoft Azure IoT. The most secure one is IBM Bluemix and AWS Platform for IoT. The most flexible one is the IBM Watson IoT Platform, while the easiest to use is Google Cloud IoT Platform.

Also, one can choose multiple platforms such as Google Cloud IoT Platform, Microsoft Azure IoT, and IBM Watson IoT Platform. In case of choosing service providers for connectivity, there are various choices:

1. APIs for AWS (Amazon Web Services)

2. APIs for Azure (Microsoft Azure)

3. APIs for IBM Bluemix

4. APIs for Google Cloud IoT Platform

5. RESTful APIs (or not)

6. HTTP REST APIs (or not)

There are many cloud-centric IOT platforms such as Amazon Web Services, IBM Bluemix, and Microsoft Azure.

They come in various categories:

1. Infrastructure as a service (IaaS)

2. Platform as a service (PaaS)

3. Software as a service (SaaS)

4. Backend as a service (BaaS)

5. Content delivery network for IOT applications

6. Firewall/security services

7. Provisioning

8. Development, hosting, and management services

9. Device management tools

Devices deployed in the cloud (e.g., in a private cloud) can be accessed by an application running on the server that hosts the service on a cloud infrastructure (e.g., on the so-called Internet infrastructure). Applications can be used to control and access such devices directly or indirectly via other applications, for example.

Since the IoT is based on the cloud, most of the platforms are cloud centric.

As the trend of IoT increases and brings a new revolution in terms of technology, security, and business model, the future IoT programs will be developed on the cloud.

Although many applications have been developed and deployed on the IoT platforms, there are some limitations to these applications:

1. The storage capacity of each device

2. The time taken (from the deployment to the completion of the application)

3. The hardware and software requirements to develop specific applications in an IoT solution as well as making full utilization of certain hardware and software components

4. Securing the applications and devices

5. Monitoring the health status of each device in the IoT program

6. Securing and monitoring the communication between each device in an IoT solution

It is important for a product manager to know the previously discussed parameters to make correct choices and assist the development team to select correct platforms.

CHAPTER 3

IoT Manager in the Agile Era

The typical process of the typical product manager in the average company is to set a plan and then lock down changes. An entirely typical scenario that you will find all over the world, if not globally then certainly locally, is that an executive wears many hats and one of those consists of being a product manager. The problem with this typical process is that it does not lend itself very well to change – and we live in a time where change is constant and unstoppable. What is required is a process that allows for changes to happen with speed and flexibility.

The reality of this world is that the consumer who controls the purse strings also has a very large say in what products, services, and features are brought to market. If you spend any time on social media, then you will quickly realize that anyone who innovates, creates, or even markets a product or service has to take into account what consumers want and will buy. The end user also dictates what everyone else will do on the planet – regardless of how they want to innovate or create.

Innovation is the act of combining two existing objects in a novel way and innovation is the relentless desire to depart from the norm and forge new paths where few have dared to go.

So how can one product manager deal with this constantly changing world? The answer lies in flexibility and agility. I have seen a product manager get so caught up in the process that they forget to be flexible and

P. Nidagundi, *The IoT Product Manager*, https://doi.org/10.1007/978-1-4842-8631-9_3

agile. As a result, they miss out on the point of being a product manager, which is to drive value to the company through innovation.

Top-down mandates will never work in this environment – especially if you are only doing it because the company is trying to burnish their image by showing corporate social responsibility (CSR).

The reason that the agile process works so well is because it allows the product manager to deal with changing market conditions and consumer demand. This is done by identifying the problem or opportunity, putting a plan in place to solve it, and then standing back in order to create change – fast, flexible, and agile. This can involve being an idea generator, idea accelerator, or delivering a product. In some instances, there is no need for anyone at all as you will be working directly with the end user (a.k.a. your customers).

The product manager is the facilitator of change – you manage the process and keep things on track to ensure that your company or organization delivers value for money. If it does not, then you have failed – simple as that. You must also take into account changes in technology and be prepared to learn new skills when required.

The agile product manager is constantly building an agile team who are looking for ways to solve a problem or provide value to their customers in the most agile way possible. They are always ready to change a plan if it does not work but will also be very quick to praise good work.

By embracing change and working with agile teams, you can quickly present value to your customers. This means that you will have new customers or retain existing ones, who will in turn buy more products or services from you. You are constantly driving growth by looking at all angles of the market, taking opportunities where they arise, and allowing your team to be agile in order to react.

There are no top-down mandates because it is you, the agile product manager, who is driving the changes by presenting them to all layers of society. You do this by constantly learning about your customers, your products and services, and how to connect them so that you can sell more.

The agile product manager is not afraid of change, nor does he fear innovation. He just takes it all in his stride, stamps his authority, and presents value to the market. He may even give you a few tips on how to be a better product manager yourself.

If you do not embrace change, then the agile product manager will outcast you from society – as will the consumer who controls your purse strings. You can't cope with change – so no one wants to buy from you. You have failed – simple as that.

3.1 IoT Product Manager Journey

Dear future IoT product manager,

Starting off as an Internet of Things product manager can be difficult. There is a lot you need to know, and a lot of things you will be facing. However, it is not impossible.

In this chapter, I discuss the journey of entering the field and some of the challenges that come with working in hardware product management. Even if your background is not in hardware, there are still plenty of lessons learned from my time as an IoT product manager that may provide insight into what you may face when starting out on your own project.

The first thing to note is that many of these problems and challenges faced by an IoT product manager are common to a lot of hardware startups. From hardware prototypes to moving into mass production, hardware products have many of the same concerns as software startups. This chapter is based on my personal experience, but the underlying problems described here are faced by most hardware product managers out there.

For the sake of this chapter, I'll use the Internet of Things (IoT) as an umbrella term for any project that involves connected hardware in some way. Martyn Currey, who was an IoT product manager at Sky when I first met him, describes it like this:

"If you spend any time with me then you'll hear me banging on about this all the time actually, [We] tend to refer to everything as IoT at Sky. So I might be working on a mobile phone app and I would say 'Oh, I'm working on an IoT app' because in my mind all apps connect to the backend somehow."

This sentiment is one that you will need to adopt if you want to call yourself a true Internet of Things product manager. It is not just about connected devices that communicate with other devices via the Internet, it is about everything! If your product has a connected device in it, then you are involved in IoT.

This definition of an Internet of Things product manager has been created to be as broad as possible, and it is what I used when I started out as an IoT product manager. Having such a broad definition of the IoT means that you will ultimately have a lot to learn. However, if you have the right attitude, then this can help accelerate your career in IoT product management because you will be able to apply all of these skills to whatever project you may be working on.

Three Practical Steps to Become an IoT Product Manager

The first step to becoming an Internet of Things product manager is to start thinking about the problems faced by IoT companies. This will give you a better idea of what it takes to deliver a successful product. By learning about these problems, you will also be able to see whether or not your skills and experiences fit with the industry you are considering entering.

The second step toward becoming an Internet of Things product manager is to learn about the best practices and standards used by companies within the industry. This will make it easier for you to work across multiple projects and problem domains. For example, a lot of IoT products use cloud-based solutions as part of their overall strategy. This means that managing how data is shared between the back end and the front end becomes a major consideration in most products.

Finally, try to get involved in an Internet of Things project as early as possible. This provides you with the chance to get some real-life experience before joining a company full time. It also means that you can use this experience to secure a job in a similar business. This sort of experience is highly sought after by many employers, so even if you don't succeed in securing a role, you will at least be able to talk about your past experiences during an interview.

3.1.1 Technology vs. Product

One of the first things that you will need to consider as an Internet of Things product manager is how you will balance your product management efforts between technology and product. There are two issues here. How much time should you spend learning about the technology vs. working on the product itself? How can you strike a balance between creating a product vision and ensuring it is technically feasible?

The first point was one that I found challenging when I started out as an IoT product manager. The important thing is to understand both sides and to make sure that you remain conscious of your role as a product manager. You should not get too bogged down in the technology side of things because you will be learning a lot as an IoT product manager. Paraphrasing my former colleague, James McNally, "To be an IoT product manager, use what you know, not what you don't know."

Another option is to spend more time thinking about the project itself instead of the technology that could potentially solve your problem. This could be anything from a mobile app to some sort of equipment or machine. If you find that your project is limited by the technology, then try and challenge this assumption. Instead, think of the problem you are working on as a product in its own right.

When it comes to deciding the technical feasibility of your idea, this is usually done by someone else. This could either be a technical cofounder or just a senior developer in your company.

3.1.2 Team and People Management

You will only succeed as an Internet of Things product manager if you can work well with others. This means that you need to spend time building relationships with the technical and nontechnical people on your team. You will also need to make your product team as efficient as possible. This is why it is important for you to know about best practices for managing a team, especially if you are starting out on your own project.

In the upcoming chapters, we discuss in detail about team and people management.

3.2 First Four Months

There has been a lot of hype around the Internet of Things (IoT) lately, and the impact that it will have on our lives in the future is hard to deny. Some estimates say that by 2025, there will be over 100 billion devices connected to each other through wireless technology, from wearables and smart lighting systems to cars. We're already starting to see smart products integrating with each other, such as a smart milk float that can tell the difference between red and white milk.

The first four months in any job are very important. The first four months as a product manager of the IoT (Internet of Things) will require you to do the following activities for your company.

As many companies are emerging in implementing IoT solutions, the need for people who have the skills and exposure to become product managers for this technology is also growing. The good thing about the IoT is that it uses existing technologies like RF, Bluetooth, Wi-Fi, and others. So there is no need to begin from scratch in any aspect of the project.

First month:

1. Get updated with the interest of the IoT in your company.

2. Understand the business and industry of the IoT.

3. Get updated on some vital keywords for the IoT implementation, like M2M (machine to machine), BLE (Bluetooth Low Energy), Wi-Fi, Zigbee, cloud IoT (platform, architecture and services), IoT monitoring system etc. Keep a notebook in which

you will list out all these keywords and when something comes up that involves any of these technologies you need to be aware about them.

4. In your first month, try to grasp the whole business process and how your product will fit into it. Your main focus should be on the learning technology and understanding end product goal.

5. Set a timeline for the business and come up with a release date (approximate) of your product or solution.

6. Identify user groups and their key concerns that need to be addressed by your product. Manage and prioritize them based on the business values (customer priorities).

Second month:

1. Identify the work that you need to do in this month.

2. Identify the gaps in your current knowledge and make a list of the things that still need to be filled up, such as target market, application of product, technology stack, verification methods, etc.

3. Take up a project that you think will enhance your understanding of the IoT. It can be a self-created project or one that is already there to study more about it.

4. Build up a checklist of the things that you need to be aware of, such as intellectual property (patents), other competing products, security and privacy concerns, etc.

5. Start thinking about the key functionalities that are needed for your product and how they will work.

6. Develop an understanding of the technology needed for your product implementation, like Bluetooth Low Energy, Zigbee, etc.

Third month:

1. In the third month, you need to start building your team.

2. Once you have got your team together, get them onboard with the product vision and understand their opinion about how the user will interact with your product.

3. If you are still working on a proof of concept for a larger project, this is the time to start working on it and make it live as soon as possible, so that your users can test it out early on and give you feedback on what they like/dislike about it.

4. In the third month, you need to identify who are your target customers and what are their needs that they are currently facing.

5. Once you have come up with a product road map and road map calendar, share it with your team and start working toward the desired outcome. This is also a good time to learn any new technology needed for your solution

Fourth month:

1. Work on various activities, such as coding and team management.

2. Involve your team in different brainstorming sessions to come up with innovative solutions and design.

3. Set up a go-live date for the product and start conducting walk-throughs for stakeholders to understand how the user will interact with the product.

4. Select any external consulting agencies that can help you in doing the product testing, analysis, and validation processes, which will help in getting the product ready for the market.

5. Plan your resources for this month.

6. At the end of the month, go through your product plan and revisit your goals, such as what you initially wanted to achieve in this month, how you fared against those goals, and if all tasks were completed. Make necessary revisions for the next month.

After the first three months:

After the first three months, if you are successful in implementing a working prototype of the IoT, or at least a proof of concept, then you can consider doing it for real scale.

3.3 Role of IoT Manager in Organizations

The Internet of Things is the only thing that can be termed as an integral part of our life from today. First, people started to use it for their convenience, and later it expanded its activities up to various other sectors like education, healthcare, and finance. It has also been adopted by many organizations for increasing efficiency in various departments and for performing tasks in real time.

It is evident from time to time that companies have a hard time retaining experienced engineers who seek new opportunities outside their comfort zones. Keeping that in mind, there are various other organizations that are looking forward to filling the vacancies by employing them in their organization. They don't have enough knowledge about how to go about the process. I am providing the information about the various roles of an Internet of Things manager that you may apply for.

We have already talked about the various needs for this position, but rather than focusing on what is needed, I will try to provide some of the most vital skills required in an ideal candidate. They are

1. **Excellent communication skills**: As the job is all about communicating with various people, you will need to possess excellent communication skills. You will be required to articulate technical concepts to nontechnical people as well. The candidate should also have a strong ability to communicate over

the phone and have good writing skills. The salary offered for this position is around $60,000 annually, depending upon the location of work, experience, and skill set of the candidate.

2. **Excellent computer skills**: It has been said that candidates applying for the job should have excellent computer skills and they should be able to use various software applications. In brief, this is the way you can look after your career growth by always staying updated with all the latest technologies.

3. **Experience in project management**: As this is a project-based job, it is highly important that you show that you can handle projects with ease as well. This is bound to be a primary factor while considering the candidate.

4. **Familiarity with APIs and RESTful Web Services**: It is very important that you have enough knowledge about the various APIs and RESTful Web Services available out there. These are used to connect various other devices with each other. You can get this information by having proper experience in the same field. It is well known that companies need more hands for this job and hence you will have to fight for your position.

5. **Strong knowledge about sensors**: It is crucial that you are experienced with the sensors as well, as you are expected to be the one who will be leading the channel of communication. You will have to be sure to use various best practices while managing

these sensors, which may not only help in detecting problems but also help in predicting them in a better manner. The salary offered for this position is around $60,000 annually, depending upon the location of work, experience, and skill set of the candidate.

6. **Familiarity with cloud computing**: As you are involved with the field of technology and are supposed to be managing the various Internet of Things devices around the globe, it is important that you have proper knowledge about the cloud computing as well. You will get in touch with various other companies or organizations, and this may help you in knowing about various new opportunities for your career growth.

7. **Strong knowledge about metrics/analytics**: This is an important role, and hence it would be very good if you could use different metrics and analytics tools effectively. You will be required to gather information about various devices and then analyze them properly. You will be responsible for presenting the whole data in a way that is easy for others to understand.

8. **Must be an excellent team player**: You need to form a good team as well, and this may help you in getting your job done more effectively. As there are limited numbers of such positions available, you need to stay competitive enough and show your prospective employers your worth.

9. **Advanced skills in cloud computing**: As you are expected to be the one who will be managing the channel of communication and the whole data, it is important that you have advanced skills in cloud computing. This is required to handle all the things efficiently and make proper use of various technologies available for it.

10. **Familiarity with various IoT device models**: It is also very important that you are familiar with various models of IoT devices as you will have to communicate these out as well while being in charge of managing device data.

11. **Must have great organizational skills**: The candidate should be a great team player, but it is also very important that they have remarkable organizational skills, as they will have to manage several things and be sure to perform up to the mark. You should be able to work toward the benefit of the whole organization as well as your own career growth.

12. **Strong confidence and strong willpower**: This can actually mean everything when it comes to this position.

3.4 IoT Product Manager Authority

The IoT product management process is an interesting one. There's no right or wrong way to do it, and there are many people who will change their process on a regular basis to adopt new best practices they hear about. The IoT product management process comes out of the software development life cycle (SDLC).

Being a product manager requires a multifaceted skill set, and IoT product management product managers need to be able to use data and analytics to inform their business decisions.

Figure 3-1 is an overview of the primary responsibilities that you will need to dedicate yourself to if you want to become an IoT product manager.

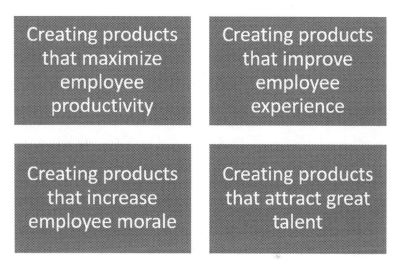

Figure 3-1. *Dedicate steps to if you want to become an IoT product manager*

1. Creating products that maximize employee productivity: IoT product managers are responsible for making sure their company's employees can work as efficiently as possible. This can be done in a number of ways, including, but not limited to, the following:

Reducing employee turnover: Companies that have positive employee turnover tend to produce better products and see increased profits. This is because the technology their employees use to do their job is streamlined and easy to use.

Streamlining processes: When processes are streamlined, employees don't waste time repeating tasks and sending emails back and forth.

Empowering employees: Empowering employees by giving them the right tools will result in better products, higher profits, and greater employee morale.

2. Creating products that improve employee experience: Empowering employees is critical to improving the business side of things, but this doesn't mean that product managers should forget about the customer. It is important to create products that make employees more efficient so they can work on their customer's product. However, it is equally important to create products that make the end user more satisfied with their product. This involves giving them the best possible experience when using your application.

3. Creating products that increase employee morale: It is important for product managers to create a positive atmosphere within their organization. Product managers should take care of their employees by doing things such as the following:

Listening to employee complaints/suggestions: Taking suggestions and feedback from employees is a great way to improve morale and make them feel important.

Empowering employees: Empowering your employees is the best way to make sure they feel valued. This can be done by providing them with the right tools to do their job and giving them the space for self-expression.

Giving recognition: Giving employees praise and recognition when they deserve it is a great way to improve morale and make them feel important.

4. Creating products that attract great talent: You can't create a great product without attracting good talent. Companies that use data science to market their products are getting better (and bigger) every year. This means that the competition for talented data scientists is increasing as well. Product managers can help their company grow by creating an environment where they are constantly surrounded by high-quality talent. Creating a positive, productive culture will go a long way toward attracting and keeping quality employees.

3.4.1 Defining Product Road Map for IoT

How to define product road map for IoT product development?

You often hear other companies' strategies for success. One such strategy is the product road map. A product road map is a strategic plan that shows how your company will meet its objectives in the future, and it's important to create one if you hope to be successful. This chapter will show you how to develop a road map for your IoT products, and also tells you how to go about implementing it.

The first thing you need to do is your IoT product development. This will require you to get the right people involved. The most important aspect of product development is user feedback, and that's why you need to create a user-centric product. You can do this by using the stakeholders, both internal and external, as well as your customers, to make sure that your product has the features needed for it to be successful. Your road map also needs to accommodate your product's business objectives.

If you think that having a road map is necessary, here's why: If you do not have a road map, you will lose the ability to measure your success in the market, which means that you won't know when to stop developing your products. If you know when to stop the development of your product, then you can have a better idea of what to do next time around. This is because you know what to improve and what features have been a success or a failure. You should also know the cost of development, which is something that a road map can be used for.

When you have your road map, it will give you a solid plan to follow in the long run. When others follow such a plan, then it gives them more motivation to continue improving in the future. It's easy to get motivated when plans are laid out clearly from the beginning (Figure 3-2).

Steps to Create a Product Road Map

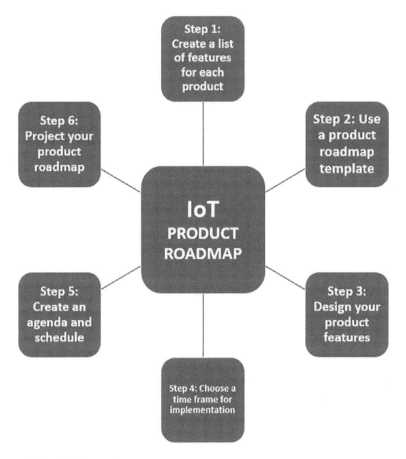

Figure 3-2. *IoT road map steps*

Step 1: Create a list of features for each product

You need to know what features are needed for your IoT product and how you will go about implementing them. You can also do this by using white papers as well as other marketing materials, such as brochures or websites. It's best to start with simple features and then ease into more complex ones. After you have the main features defined, then you should map them out in scenarios.

Step 2: Use a product road map template

You can find templates that you can use as a guide for your development on the Internet. The Internet is full of them, and you should have no problem finding one that fits your needs. Just make sure that you choose one that's relevant to your product or service. You may also want to hire a professional to help you create your road map.

Step 3: Design your product features

To design your features, you should first think about how the service will be available to the clients. Also, think about how it will be used. Once you have that done, then it's time to go through each feature and make sure that it's relevant and needed for your IoT product.

Step 4: Choose a time frame for implementation

You have to decide how long it will take to implement your features. This is important because it helps you set your deadlines and lets you know when the features should be done by. If they are not, then they will not be included in the road map. When you're creating your road map, remember that the features may need to be prioritized. This means that some features will need to be implemented earlier than others. There are project timeline and milestones that you can use with the road map, such as a year or a quarter. You can choose whichever one fits best with your product.

Step 5: Create an agenda and schedule

Once you know when your product will be ready and how it will work, then it's time to create an agenda and set a schedule that applies to all the features. This will help you know when you will implement different features. The schedule will also tell you when to meet with the stakeholders and how often that should happen.

Step 6: Project your product road map

Once you have your schedule and agenda set, then it's time to put it all together in a project management software. The software will allow you to create a visual of what you want to achieve, so that you know where they need to be by the given date.

In short: When it comes to product development, it's important for you to know how to develop your road map. When you have a road map, you will know when to stop implementing certain features and can use the road map accordingly.

3.4.2 Need Of Comprehensive Product Metrics and Quantitative Measurement Structure

The industrial Internet of Things (IoT) is a revolution that's changing the way business runs. The industrial Internet-enabled businesses can get information about the in-plant condition and other data, collect data that is useful for making decisions, and create action plans to address any issues before they lead to downtime or significant operational problems. As businesses are embracing the IoT these days, they are faced with some challenges while trying to evolve into an IoT company.

The Internet of Things (IoT) is a network of devices that are connected to each other via the Internet Protocol. These devices can communicate with each other using the Internet or LAN. They are also capable of receiving and transmitting data. As more devices and systems connect to the Internet, businesses require a comprehensive metrics platform for managing them. The Internet of Things has applications in numerous industries such as healthcare, education, smart cities, multifamily housing, and many more. The Internet of Things product manager is responsible for ensuring that the company's goals are met.

The primary job of the IoT product manager is to develop a comprehensive strategy for all the IoT solutions. This person identifies and evaluates all the options on different solutions and products available in the market. After evaluating their options, an IoT product manager should then decide what exactly would be needed to achieve their established goals and objectives as per their business needs and desired result. The person should also be aware of their short-term and long-term objectives and what the impact of product strategy will be on it. The next step is to evaluate the competitive performance of each product/solution. After that, the individual needs to make a decision on which solution to go with, based on their assessed requirements.

How to Develop Comprehensive Product Metrics and Quantitative Measurement Structure?

The IoT product manager should develop metrics that are useful in evaluating the performance of each solution. The product metrics for an IoT solution should be developed by analyzing the old as well as new metrics. A product metric is one that helps the company have a better understanding on how a particular solution will change their company. The IoT product manager can also develop other measurable data based on the context of their business needs and goals.

The method used to develop metrics should be the one that is easy and quick. The decision to use certain metrics has to be made based on the risks associated with them. It is important for the product manager to have data about whether or not it is possible for each solution being considered by them to meet their goals and objectives. The IoT product manager should also develop a strategy on how they are going to achieve their goals based on the data gathered from various solutions.

The IoT product manager should also be able to identify risks associated with each strategy being considered and what plans have been put in place to create a system or a process to reduce them. The plan should also be made in case the systems/processes that have been created are not effective. The set of metrics for an IoT solution can be different depending on their purpose and objectives.

Steps in Developing Product Metrics and Quantitative Measurement Structure

Step 1: Define all the stakeholders.

Step 2: Define the company's goals and objectives.

Step 3: Define the metrics that are needed to achieve the company's goals and objectives. The IoT product manager should be able to get data from various sources such as internal team, external team, vendors, and others.

Step 4: Evaluate all the possible solutions or products that can help in achieving the set of metrics for their solution.

Step 5: Develop a comprehensive strategy that fulfills the company's goals and objectives.

The IoT product manager should be able to develop a comprehensive product metrics for their solution by integrating all the components of an IoT solution. In order to do so, they have to understand the different components of an IoT solution and how they can be used to deliver an entire system. The main aim behind developing the product metrics is to evaluate the performance of each individual solution in its own context.

The IoT product manager should be able to identify and understand the right metrics and which metrics would be best suited for their goal.

Step 1: The first step is to define all the stakeholders of an IoT solution. The main stakeholders of an IoT solution include the user, product manager, implementer, application or system owner, tester, and other stakeholders of the company.

Step 2: The next step is to define the metrics that are required to achieve the objectives. These objectives should be based on the overall goals of the company. It is important for the IoT product manager to have a deep understanding of their business needs and goals.

Step 3: The third step is to evaluate all the possible solutions or products that can help the company achieve their objectives. The IoT product manager should be able to understand how each solution or product would fit in with their business needs, team requirements, and others.

Step 4: The fourth step is to develop a strategy for the company. The IoT product manager should be able to develop a robust strategy that will ensure that their goals are met.

The purpose of the product metrics is to evaluate the performance of the solution. It is also used in evaluating how well each problem or issue would be solved by each option.

Product metrics help the business owners in making decisions on which solution would be most suitable for them depending on their context.

3.4.3 Importance Of Implements Reporting Dashboards

In this we discuss about reporting dashboards for managers and its importance of integrating technology into your business activity. Reporting dashboards provides a great deal of insight on how to create and run a successful IoT project, as well as how to manage the data that is collected. This chapter will introduce you not just to our company's field and market but also to some key practices that you should be implementing in order to get the best results possible with this kind of project.

The initial step in your IoT project is to define the report that needs to be created. This will serve as a learning tool for your employees who have been hired to work on it. It will also serve as another form of communication between the company and its customers and clients. Next, it's important to understand what kind of data a report should contain; you can download the right templates. You'll want to create something that can help you determine your unique strategy and tactics when it comes to designing projects like this one.

The report has to contain information about the project, so that you and your team know what kind of data you are collecting about all the various aspects of your IoT project. Understanding the reports will also help you to think about all the things that you need to consider, like working with a vendor or business partner. This is very important because it helps you to define how to set up your own business relationships as well. You will be able to measure your progress against both internal and external goals as well.

It's recommended that you show the report to your higher management rather than just giving the report to them. This way, you will be able to discuss the information with them and ask for their feedback. In order for this data to be useful, it has to be presented in a way that everyone can understand; you will have to look into the best ways that other companies are getting their data out there.

You must be very careful and monitor the IoT system because it is a strong part of your business and you have to show that you are interested in it. If you don't have a tracking system and the data isn't being shown to you, then you will struggle to see what's happening with your project.

Creating a Report for Higher Management

The report for higher management should contain the high level analytical information that you've collected from your project. You can add the current trends with your project and future projection, planning or possibilities. Based on you report management able to make effective decisions.

Getting Started with an Internet of Things Project

One of the most important things that you have to do is to understand why you are doing this in the first place. This will help your team to see exactly what they are supposed to be doing and what their purpose is in working on this project. Keep in mind that it is important for your team to find out why you are doing this so that they can understand the purpose of the project.

Setting Up IoT Project Manager Work Flow

In order to make this happen, you will have to determine how you are going to design your setup. In order to do this, you will have to talk with your vendors and ask them what kind of things they are going to be able to provide. You'll be able to decide what kind of things you're going to use, like the hardware, and how it's going to be set up. It is also very important that you keep track of this because it will help you to see how your network and your team are doing.

As a business owner, the most important thing that you have to do is keep up with the latest information that is going on in the market. You will have to be constantly updating yourself, so that you can make sure that this project is all right. You should create a meeting with your team, so that they can get started on this project. Be sure to understand exactly what you want them to do and how long it is going to take. You can also tell them what kind of data you want them to track, so they know where they're supposed to focus their energies.

It's vital that you keep all of this data safe, because if you lose it, then there's no way that you'll be able to track down your progress and know where this project stands.

Implementing Reporting Dashboards

You'll want to develop a reporting dashboard that allows you to get a good understanding of the data that is being tracked. You will also have to make sure that you have someone in your company who can focus on monitoring all the data and help you to make sense of it. Having this kind of information at your fingertips is going to allow you to see everything at once, so it's important that you know exactly what you're looking for when this kind of data comes in.

The Questions to Ask Yourself

Are you able to see the data that the company is collecting? Is this the data or information that you need to be tracking? Are you able to easily understand what is being collected and how? Knowing these things will help you become a better business owner and in order to make sure that everything is going according to plan.

To get started, you'll need an easy-to-understand report template. This will help you to design the report for your company, so that you can get started on your project right away. It's important that this is easy to understand so that everyone can see what is being collected. If it's too confusing, then it makes it even harder to use these reports to improve your network and your business.

Once you have the report template ready to go, then you'll need a system in place. You can build your own system, but it's recommended that you find a business partner who will be able to build and design this for you. That way, you won't have to worry about the technical aspects and how the information is being collected, because the company you work with will handle that for you.

The next thing that is important to monitor is how your customers are responding. If they're not happy with your product, then you'll have to go back and reevaluate. This is very important because you don't want to lose customers by having a bad product. You'll have to make sure that the people who are using the product are enjoying it and that they are getting what they want out of this IoT project.

The next thing that you need to do is set up a meeting with your team and with your suppliers. This will be the first time that you're going to be able to see how everything is working together and how everything is being received. This can help your team to make the right decisions when it comes to the future of their project and their business.

You may want to invest in a small data analysis tool, such as a spreadsheet or Excel, if you are only collecting simple data. If you have more complex requests, then it's recommended that you use a more professional tool such as Tableau or QlikView.

If your operation is small, then it's usually going to be best to invest in a single device that will be able to handle all of the data collecting that you need it to do. If you are a larger company, then you may want to invest in multiple devices that can handle this for you.

Investing in a professional report template is something that will help you greatly. It's important that the template is easy to understand and easy for people who are not involved in web development or data analysis to use.

You will want to install your report template, so that you can start working on your reports. It's important that everyone is able to get the information they need and be able to use the information that they are looking for within a few minutes. You'll need someone who has experience in data analysis and web development, but it's recommended that you hire a company to do this for you.

A good way of tracking everything would be through an account like Google Analytics or Piwik. This can help you to keep track of the data that your company has collected and used. You will be able to tell what is being done with the data that is being collected. The great thing about these programs is that they are very easy to use, so it's not going to be hard for anyone who's working on this project, to get started right away.

You will also want to make sure that you put together a list of data requirements before you start working with your team of web developers, data analysts, and graphic designers. This will help you to develop a plan of action and ensure that everything is going according to plan.

Make sure that you are checking your network on a consistent basis. This is essential because your system can easily break and then there will be no way for you to understand exactly what is going on within your business. It's important that you know what the status of your network is, so if anything goes wrong, then you'll know instantly.

It's important that you are able to monitor the data that is being collected because if it's not in your network and you don't know about it, then there is going to be no way for you to make sure that your business is using the data correctly. This means that if nothing has changed in the past week, then there is no way of knowing what this data can reveal.

In short, think first for whom you are creating report and what kind of data we are collecting.

3.4.4 Partnering Closely with Key Stakeholders to Optimize Overall Product Adoption and Performance-Driven Growth

The Internet of Things (IoT) is the name for the rapidly evolving world where physical objects are connected to the Internet. The IoT has fueled the next industrial revolution that's now underway, affecting business models and changing how companies connect with their customers. There are three levels of connectivity between things and people, as follows:

---

1. Device-to-device communication

2. Device-to-cloud communication

3. Device-to-home network communication

The Internet of Things manager (IoTM) is a new role that helps companies deliver the promises of the IoT. It involves driving innovation, making products more useful, and using data to meet customer demands. Your role will be to lead product management and development in the IoT organization. You'll have the opportunity to bring your passion for technology to a large organization and to help impact billions of lives. The IoT manager will be responsible for creating and managing IoT products.

How does a product manager partner closely with key stakeholders to optimize overall product adoption and performance-driven growth?

1. **Lead cross-functional teams**: To lead a team, you must develop deep expertise in the product area. You must understand the needs and wants of your customer base and how your product fits into their lives. You need to be able to align your team with overall business goals and communicate a vision of where the market is going. You have to have enough business acumen to understand how your product will contribute to the organization's long-term objectives.

2. **Develop strategy**: To develop a strategy, you'll need to understand how your product will fit into the market. You'll also need to understand your company's strengths and weaknesses. Your goal will be to develop an innovative strategy that can help your company capitalize on new opportunities as competitors respond and technology advances.

3. **Define features and functions**: The IoT manager will define what customer needs a product must address. He will lead the team in defining the attributes of the product, such as its size, shape, and user interface. The IoT manager will also define how the product will function. The IoT manager will work with the software developers, interface designers, and other product managers to define exactly how customers will interact with the product and what it can do.

4. **Integrate with existing systems**: The IoT manager will have to work closely with existing systems. This involves working with sales and marketing to determine how the new product will fit into a customer's life cycle. For example, if the product is sold to companies that sell products to other companies, or has advertising features, this will affect its business model. He will work with operations to determine how the product will be produced. The IoT manager must also work with the sales team and the company's resellers to help them understand the product, its features, and when it will be available.

5. **Develop plans for managing time and resources**: You'll have to give careful consideration to your time allocation. The IoT manager will usually spend a considerable amount of time meeting with customers, reporting on progress, and working with the marketing department to determine new product offerings. You'll also need to devote time to developing new products and maintaining existing ones. You'll work with the product management team to develop plans for managing time and resources.

6. **Take advantage of a new product strategy**: This involves using an existing product as a basis for a new one. For example, you might create an entirely new product based on the success of an existing one. Or you might use aspects of your existing products in conjunction with new ones in order to deliver more value to your customers than before.

7. **Monitor competitors and the changing market**: The IoT manager will need to keep up with new developments in the industry. You'll want to follow industry trends and identify areas for growth. You'll need to know how your competitors are performing, where they're strong, and where they're weak. This will help you develop a strategy that has the greatest chance of success.

8. **Keep customers up to date with new developments**: The IoT manager will want to present your company's offerings in the best possible light. You'll need to keep customers up to date on changes, delays, and other issues. This helps them see the product as a dynamic offering that's always improving and keeps them interested in purchasing your product over those of your competitors.

9. **Develop a plan for dealing with a crisis**: The IoT manager will need to develop a crisis preparedness plan that addresses issues such as unanticipated product failure and theft. You'll want to work with the legal department and other departments to define what your company's policies are regarding such matters and how they'll be enforced.

10. **Provide regular reports on progress**: The IoT manager will have to report regularly on the progress of the product. This includes reports to management, which will be used to determine whether or not to continue funding the project. This can be difficult, because real-world testing doesn't

always match predictions. You may lose some credibility with your stakeholders if you continually overstate the potential of a product.

11. **Develop a vision for the product**: The IoT manager will have to develop a vision for the product that is both clear and compelling. This includes identifying which customers will be best served with which features and how the product will contribute to a company's overarching strategy. Through this, you can determine whether to invest in the project or if an alternative should be considered.

12. **Develop a plan for execution**: The IoT manager will have to come up with a plan for how the product is to be executed. This includes defining who will do what and when and how the features will be delivered. You'll also need to define how problems are handled and what steps are taken when key customers are unhappy with the product.

13. **Develop project goals**: You'll also have to determine what kinds of results the product is expected to achieve. You'll need to check with your customers and other stakeholders to determine whether the deliverables are what they want. This will help you define project goals and ensure that you're meeting your own expectations.

14. **Define project tasks**: You'll also have to come up with the appropriate tasks for each phase of the project. This includes creating a timeline for each step and determining which departments will be

responsible for what. You may need to hire more employees or partner with others, depending on the scope of the project.

15. **Develop a plan for ensuring compliance with regulations**: Finally, you'll have to develop a plan for complying with applicable regulations. For example, some products need to be CE certified before they can legally be sold in the European Union. This means that you'll need to work with your legal department to ensure that your product complies with applicable legislation.

16. **Develop a plan for managing costs**: The IoT manager will also have a financial and budgeting component to the position. This will include deciding which resources are required, what the necessary capital expenditures are, and when they'll need to be paid. You'll also have to determine whether you can pay for additional employees or if outside funding will have to be sought.

17. **Develop a plan for management of personnel and training**: You'll also have a number of issues relating to managing personnel. This can range from ensuring that your team members have the necessary skills to ensuring that they're properly trained and paid. You'll also want to prepare a plan for managing changes in personnel and address any related issues.

18. **Define approved use of technology**: The IoT manager will also have to define how your company will use certain technologies.

3.4.5 IoT Manager End-to-End Development

The Internet of Things (IoT) is a revolutionary technology that has been deployed over the past few years to create systems that can track and monitor almost anything in the context of everyday life. However, to set up these systems, companies need to hire product managers who are responsible for overseeing the development of both ongoing training for direct and indirect customers for use of the IoT products.

As part of building an IoT product, a company will produce training materials that may be meant only for internal use or public access online. This training material is meant to provide users with information about the product and how to use it, as well as how to troubleshoot and modify the product. The training marked for user guides, written in text or audio formats, will probably be given to the product manager or his staff.

Skills Needed by a Product Manager

The skills needed by a product manager are very similar to those found in any other professional capacity. However, a product manager in the IoT must also be skilled in IT, software development, and programming language. While this isn't necessary for every product manager in an organization, a product manager is expected to be familiar with the technology and APIs used in their system. This will give them the ability to provide support for users if needed.

As a product manager, it's useful to have personal familiarity with common systems like Microsoft Excel and SQL Server Management Studio. Product managers are also expected to be skilled in the use of cloud computing platforms and security, network architecture, and wireless networking. The Internet of Things is not a process; it's a collection of technologies that work together to allow for devices to connect and exchange information.

Responsibilities of a Product Manager

As a product manager, it's your responsibility to oversee all stages of development until the product is delivered as well as ensure users are able to use the product correctly. Once the product has been deployed, it's your job to monitor usage and ensure customers are receiving the value they expect.

The majority of a product manager's time will be spent communicating with clients and other staff members in order to determine how the product should operate and what features it should have. This communication may include asking clients what they'd like to see in the IoT project, as well as making sure they understand why certain changes need to be made. Once changes are made to the product, it's your responsibility to continue those changes until they're complete and ready to be released.

In the process of communication, a product manager may also be asked to evaluate if a product is worthy of being released or if it needs more work before it can be sent to production. A product manager will also have the opportunity to ensure software development has been completed as well as identifying areas that need additional attention before release. This will include determining if features need to be included in the system that were not included in the beta test.

A product manager must also be able to communicate with employees from other departments and have them understand how the IoT project will affect their daily tasks and operations. This is a necessary part of outreach as well as showing appreciation for their work on the project. Understanding how a project can benefit each employee and department will help prevent real problems from arising.

Lastly, a product manager might have training to provide IP connectivity for users. The training may be limited to an actual product release or it may cover helping employees understand how to use the IoT product. Either way, the product manager is in charge of ensuring users are able to complete the initial setup to work with the product.

Competencies Needed by a Product Manager

To be a successful product manager, it helps if you have a bachelor's degree in computer science, software engineering, or information technology. Having a degree in one of these fields will ensure you're knowledgeable enough to understand the technology being used in the project.

While a product manager doesn't need to be technical, they should be familiar with the technologies being used. You need to be familiar with this in order to explain the rationale behind the design choices you made for the IoT device. It also helps when you have some understanding of what challenges may occur with implementing a new feature or applying an update to existing functionality.

In addition to understanding a technical topic well, it's important to be able to communicate that understanding in a way that's easy to understand. It takes training and practice, but this is an important skill to develop as it will help reduce friction between employees when discussing changes being made.

Managing the Software Development Teams

Product managers are responsible for making sure the product is developed correctly, but where does the responsibility begin? As a product manager, you may be in charge of a team of developers or a project manager managing multiple teams. This will depend on the size and complexity of the product being developed. In either case, it's important you understand your role as it pertains to handling software development.

The most common area of responsibility for a product manager is overseeing how software development is completed and how it affects their project. This includes monitoring communication between software development teams and the product manager they're working with. The product manager should also review team meeting minutes and make sure everyone understands when a change needs to be made or why a certain approach was taken.

The product manager should take part in technical discussions which will ensure they understand how the product will be developed. This will help when discussing timelines, reduction of functionality, or changes to requirements during the software development process.

Another important part of the product manager's role is monitoring the software development process to ensure it stays on track. This should include analyzing estimates for new features and compatibility testing for existing features. It's also important to communicate changes to timelines with clients and other stakeholders in order to ensure the project will be completed on time.

Communicating with Customers

As a product manager, you'll be responsible for communicating with clients as well as other staff members. This includes considering how changes may change the project and how those changes affect all stakeholders. It's important you understand the business and technical needs for the project to ensure any alterations being made will be beneficial for everyone.

When it comes to communicating, a product manager will work with project managers and other staff members in order to discuss how an update or addition might affect the end-user experience. They might also play a role in how changes affect the project schedule, so it's important to understand the intricacies of software development.

Product managers should also be able to communicate changes that are being made to clients in a timely manner. They might work with their software development team to determine why a change is needed and if there's any impact to timelines or other aspects of development. This will enable the client to anticipate features being added or changes being made, so it can be incorporated into their road map.

Taking Part in Quality Assurance Testing

Quality assurance is an important role for product managers. This testing procedure will ensure the product is implemented correctly and everyone who depends on it knows how to use it. When conducting testing, product managers should know what to test for and make sure any appropriate tests are run for all components of the product's functionality.

One of the most important parts of quality assurance is making sure no bugs or errors are present. This includes evaluating code, user interfaces, and data models to ensure nothing has been overlooked. This testing procedure can help identify issues before the product becomes public and it begins to be used by clients.

Since bugs can slip through the cracks during quality assurance, product managers should understand how their software development team follows up on reported bugs and issues. This can help identify ways to reduce the number of issues being presented and make sure they get resolved in a timely manner.

It's also important to test the software that's developed so it works as expected. Product managers should ensure there are no conflicts with existing software or other installed applications before their product is deployed for use. It's important to consider whether any additional testing will be required if their product is used alongside other products and services.

Establishing a Go-to-Market Strategy

The final area of product management that's important for IoT professionals to understand is the role they have in communicating product features and attributes to the end user. The product manager should work with designers and developers in order to establish a go-to-market strategy. This can include how the product will be marketed, including if it will be sold through an existing platform or if marketing campaigns will be created by the team responsible for developing it.

There are several methods for going to market for a new or updated product, including designing a website or creating an app specifically for the product. It's important the company understands which method is most appropriate and is compatible with their product as well as software and hardware companies they want to work with. They should also consider how much money they'll need to invest in marketing and advertising in order to promote the product.

The guidance of a product manager will help determine how the product will be marketed, so it's important they're familiar with common marketing strategies. This can include running prerelease customer surveys to determine end-user interest before a product is introduced to the public. The results of the survey should be considered when finding partners to work with and determining how the product manager will communicate the product.

Product managers should also understand the budget that's involved with marketing, as this will help determine how much money should be allocated to their product. They can also use any previous results from surveys or brand research to determine how their target audience might respond to the product. This information can be used when creating a go-to-market strategy and determining how the company will advertise or market the product.

If the company is using a third party to market their product, the product manager will work with them to come up with promotional strategies. This can include suggestions for how the third party can market the product on social media and other websites. This is especially important if there are social media influencers that might be able to promote an IoT product. It's important to understand what type of content they might share, who might share it, and how these people are selected.

Creating a Sales and Marketing Plan

Once the product is ready to be launched, it's important to have a go-to-market strategy. This involves creating a plan that establishes how the team will publicize the product and how they'll convince potential clients to purchase it.

One of the first steps in creating a sales and marketing plan is determining who will be responsible for promoting the product. For example, if a company has an existing website, they might include further information about their products on that website. If they don't have a website, they might create a user manual or other information that can be used to explain how the product works.

After the go-to-market strategy is established, it's time to create a sales and marketing plan. This will include what tasks the team will be responsible for when promoting the product, including activities like writing chapters and giving presentations at conferences. The company will also need to spend time building connections with potential customers and clients so everyone who's important knows about their product.

CHAPTER 4

IoT Product Development and Life Cycle

There are seven steps in IoT product development:

1. **Identify the market opportunities and needs**
   (usually in a research phase): In the first phase, the
   market research process and survey are used in
   order to identify the real needs or problems of the
   customer/users. In a research phase, the product
   might be developed by a consultant rather than an
   in-house team. This is time consuming and resource
   intensive.

   In order to reduce this time, the product can be
   designed using an iterative design process (typically
   done once every week), which involves looking
   at previous designs, then creating changes based
   on what users have said they want. This way, you
   can develop the product as quickly and efficiently
   as possible, as you can see what users like/dislike
   about your current design.

© Padmaraj Nidagundi 2022
P. Nidagundi, *The IoT Product Manager*, https://doi.org/10.1007/978-1-4842-8631-9_4

2. **Create a business model that is robust enough to support developing the product**: Building an IoT device is expensive, so it needs funding in order to be made. These funds can come from venture capitalists (VC), banks, investment crowdfunding, friends and family, or grants.

   The first two options are generally for large companies or organizations who can also afford to sell their product at a premium. Friends and family are more likely to invest in you because they know you, so this is a better option for small startups. Grants can be a good option if you're looking for seed funding, but these are harder to get than loans from banks or friends/family.

   Another option for funding the device is to find a win-win partnership, where the organization gives you funding in exchange for a certain amount of equity (stock) in your company.

   For example, Microsoft invested $2 million in Cambridge Silicon Radio (CSR), which developed a Bluetooth headset. This resulted in CSR developing a cheaper Bluetooth headset that they could sell to Nokia and other manufacturers.

   The third option is an investment crowdfunding platform. These platforms are used by companies to raise money for their ideas and/or for the development of their products. They may ask for a percentage stake of your company in return for funding or simply ask for a cash sum. Once the amount of investment needed has been calculated, investments can be made, ranging from a few thousands to tens of thousands of pounds (USD). Generally, the larger the number of investors you have, the better your chances are at getting funded.

Research shows that the majority of investments made in IoT startups are done so by early adopters who are interested in what the startups are doing. It is worth keeping in mind, though, that crowdfunding isn't an easy way to get funding for a project or company. You need to have a professional website and good marketing skills.

3. **Design and build an IoT device**: The design process takes time and effort, especially if you know little about electronics or hardware.

One way of doing this is to contract an external company that has the experience and skill set to help you develop your product. Another way is to use online communities such as Thingiverse, where users share open source hardware designs, or Instructables, where users share instructions on how to build several different products (e.g., lamps, USB chargers, etc.).

If you have a limited budget, it's worth trying all the preceding methods in order to save time and money.

The cheapest option is to use online communities, but this could take longer than working with an external company or using your own knowledge.

4. **Sell or deploy on an IoT platform**: Once your product has been created, you then need a platform to deploy it on. There are many different types of platforms available: web, mobile, and cloud-based services. The platforms connect devices to the Internet and allow communication between the device and other electronic devices. Using these platforms means that you can easily share information with other devices or users. For example, you could connect your IoT device to your computer and then share the data on a social networking site, such as Twitter or Facebook.

Depending on what platform you use, there will be different ways of accessing the data. For example, you could use a website that displays all the data produced by your device(s). Alternatively, you could build an application (app) for a mobile platform (e.g., Android) or a downloadable application for a tablet device.

5. **Develop new features after initial release**: This is where you will add new features to your product and perhaps improve upon it in order to make it better and more user-friendly.

   In order to introduce new features, you will have to make changes. After a new version of the product has been released, you will have to get feedback from customers so that you can use this as a way of making improvements and adding features such as the following:

   An update to the existing device design to make it more user-friendly.

   A new feature or three for your product.

   A change in the market (e.g., increase in demand, decrease in demand, new competition).

   A change in the product's pricing structure.

   A change in the product's support model.

   It is very important to get feedback from customers and users so that you can make changes to your product as fast as possible.

   Devices with cloud-based platforms often have an API. This API allows users to access data from the device and/or interact with it. The API is basically a set of commands that you can use to interact with your device, for example, in order to get data or send information to the device.

For example, if you have built an app for a tablet device which tracks data from your IoT device, you could then use an API to send information to that app.

6. **Improve IoT device**: Once this is done, your product is ready to be released. Unlike with other types of products, testing many IoT devices in the market is not straightforward.

    For example, you might want to test it on a specific type of land to see how it will do in certain conditions (e.g., sandy soil, rocky soil) or how a certain kind of weather might affect its performance (e.g., rain).

    It would be difficult to do this without the system being connected to a real-world environment. However, you could use a simulator to test it in a virtual environment.

    With the help of an IoT device, you could then set up several scenarios in your test lab and experiment with different sensors to see how they might affect the performance of your product. If your product is sold via an online platform, you can make use of simulations such as Simulated Environmental Chamber, which allows you to replicate many different weather patterns and temperatures indoors. Using IoT to gather data, you could then simulate and test different conditions (e.g., temperature) in order to track the performance of your device and then use this information to improve upon it.

7. **Further considerations**: You also need to consider your communication model when deploying an IoT solution into your business.

The communication model is a set of rules, models, and procedures that are used to connect your product or service to the users. This can include making use of social media such as Twitter, Facebook, and LinkedIn. There are also many additional factors that you should consider when it comes to deployment, such as customer communication models, network design, and product support.

An IoT project is made up of software components: devices, servers, back end, and analytics. These components can be hosted on cloud-based platforms, on-premises systems, or a hybrid of the two.

An IoT system is designed to collect and transmit data from sources such as sensors, electronic devices like computers, and storage.

One of the main benefits of IoT is its ability to store, manage, and process this data in real time. This can then be used to make decisions about how things are done (e.g., manufacturing automation), improve decision making (e.g., consumer habits), and reduce waste (e.g., energy).

It is also worth noting that IoT networks are often spread over a large geographical area or, in some cases, the world (e.g., a large building).

This can be problematic because of the issue of latency in data transfer. This is when the time taken for data to reach its destination increases to such an extent that it becomes unusable. There are two main reasons why this might happen:

1. **Network and device latency**: This is when a device's (e.g., sensor) data gets transmitted to the network and then sent across to other networks. The latencies for these different networks (i.e., cellular, Wi-Fi) will vary depending on the size of each one and how close they are (i.e., cell towers, access points).

2. **Server latency**: This is when data gets transmitted
    from the network to the server, where it is
    transferred and stored. This usually takes longer
    than the other latency factor because it involves
    transferring data from multiple devices (i.e., two
    endpoints, one for each device; endpoints are
    standard components of a connected device).

The main factors that can affect network and server latency are
distance and congestion. When data gets transferred over a network, it
also needs to be processed by computer systems and then sent to other
systems. This can result in additional delays.

This is why it's important to consider the performance of your data
collection, transmission, and storage systems in terms of latency before
attempting to use them.

Although there may be some instances where IoT data cannot be
processed in real time (e.g., during device setup, when updating the
system), it is important that the data transfer is as fast as possible so that
IoT devices can perform optimally at all times.

Another point worth making here is that latency can really benefit
certain business sectors more than others.

For example, an IoT application designed to monitor home energy
consumption activity could have a latency of just a few seconds, whereas a
grocery delivery company will not be able to benefit from this.

This is because it's far easier to deliver produce in remote areas within
minutes than it is to install sensors in thousands of homes.

Some companies also consider the effect that latency has on
performance. In many cases, for instance, enterprise systems are more
"robust" than consumer-oriented applications. This is because they
tend to be developed with greater attention to security, privacy, and
performance requirements.

It will, therefore, be important for your company to consider how it might limit the impact of latency on performance when implementing an IoT project.

There are a number of strategies that can be employed in order to deal with latency:

1. **Streaming**: This can be used in a number of situations and works by collecting data from a system (e.g., a sensor) and then performing a process or calculation (e.g., a mathematical formula) to make it fit into a particular stream of data that is being sent across the network. The data can be sent to a local device (e.g., a PC) that can then store it, or sent to the cloud for further processing and storage. This can, therefore, help to speed up the process of transferring data from one device to another (i.e., from one system to another).

2. **Replication**: The process of replicating data is when it is copied and sent to a number of systems. This can be done in real time or via batch processes (i.e., storing data in bulk) and can also be used to ensure that data gets replicated across different devices (e.g., multiple PCs).

3. **Edge-wise processing**: This is where the process involves transferring and processing the data at an edge, before sending it across the network to its final destination.

4. **Filtering**: This is the process where data is gathered and then used to filter out useless information. This can help to speed up the transmission of data and make it easier to process when it reaches its destination.

This has been a very summary of latency issues in IoT, but if you want to learn more about this, I recommend reading this chapter on the subject.

In summary, there are many aspects that need to be taken into account when planning your IoT deployment (e.g., network, device, system), and you need to understand the types of latencies that are possible before you start.

4.1 IoT Development Life Cycle

IoT products are subject to many types of devices that need management over their life cycle. It's important to plan out the life cycle of your IoT product and understand what you need to do; you can make your IoT product better. This chapter will give you an explanation of the five phases of the IoT product life cycle and provide a checklist for each phase. It will help you plan out your IoT product's life cycle so it can achieve its full potential!

Nine Phases of IoT Product Development Life Cycle

> **Ideation and prototyping**: In this phase, hardware and software integrated, and the first prototype model is created. Product ideation is building a blueprint of your final product by creating a rough model.

> **Development stage**: In this phase, the team takes the prototype and build it into a fully integrated version. This is where you'll be doing hardware configuration, software integration and development, and integration of additional hardware components. Prototyping is the process of creating a prototype of a product before it is ready to be sold. It involves testing the product and its design to find out if it can work as planned.

Design and development: In this phase, actual design is created, software and hardware are integrated, and product is tested and released to the market. IoT design and development is a combination of art and science. It is a process of creating a new product from the concept to the actual finished product. Operation is when your IoT product is out in the open, in use, and it's being used by people. This phase involves monitoring and analyzing how your product is being used by customers. It involves collecting information about how your IoT products are being used, what features they like most, what features they don't like, etc. There are several tools you can use to do this.

Provision and deploy: In this phase, companies develop and supply hardware to end users and provide services to customers. The product is produced in large quantities for market acceptance and user testing. Provision and deploy is actually the last phase, but it is done at the beginning of the product life cycle. This is where your IoT product is built and ready to be sold and distributed in large quantities.

Manage and monitor: In this phase, companies can manage and monitor the product from a central location. It is possible to gather customer feedback on the product and make adjustments accordingly.

Scaling and growth: This phase is for further developing and improving your IoT product. It involves planning scale out of your product, scaling out the application, the cost associated with scale, and engineering to support it when the amount of data goes up dramatically.

Update and maintain: In this phase, customer feedback is gathered to make the product more user-friendly, safe, and reliable. The IoT product's life cycle has come to an end.

Commercialization: In this phase, the team makes a large investment in taking your idea into reality by buying off-the-shelf products and creating customized devices or software to fit your needs. In next step make sure that these tools are compatible with your existing buildings and surroundings, and your product isn't just cool but can be practical for the intended use.

Maintenance: In this phase, you'll be handling customer service and fixing bugs on any of your products that need it. This phase is like a pit stop for your IoT products between production runs. It involves handling customer complaints, improving design flaws, and building additional functionality into your device's software or firmware.

After you have completed the product design, development, and release to end user, the product is ready to start! You will need to get feedback from your users.

Step 1: Find out a good feedback from your users.

Some of the ways to find out a good feedback are online users' reviews, consumers' comments, and suppliers' and developers' suggestions.

Step 2: Make your product as user-friendly as possible by improving functionality. For instance, you can add some hot keys for making menus more visual for user interaction. Also, follow the user's feedback to ensure that your product has all the good features.

Step 3: Product testing

During product testing, you can run some performance tests and build a rudimentary version of your app with a minimum amount of components.

Step 4: Release and marketing

After receiving the feedback from testers to improve your product, it's time to release it.

You will need to set up a website for sales and marketing. You will also need to do some marketing for the product.

Step 1: Make a list of all the devices that you want to connect to your core product.

Step 2: Ensure your device is connected to the Internet and can be accessed from anywhere.

Step 3: Define your success factors for each device.

Step 4: Test your systems for working together.

Step 5: Analyze the data to see if it matches with the success factors.

Step 6: Run a marketing campaign.

Step A: Start up digital marketing.

Step B: Go live with your product.

Step C: Continue to keep updating and improving your product as time goes on.

After the product is available, you will need to ensure its security and manage it properly. Review important parts of the product in detail, such as the product interface or customer management system, and see what you can improve in each one.

Step 1: Review your current sales and traffic to find out what you can improve.

Step 2: Set up a new digital marketing campaign.

Step 3: Keep managing your product by optimizing the user interface.

You can follow this simple template to keep track of your IoT product's life cycle. This template has all the necessary steps required for successful development, from idea validation to launching it on the market.

4.2 IoT Product Evaluation Metrics

Product management is the process of developing, launching, and managing new products. It is a challenging role, not only because there are many different perspectives that must be considered in order to make the right decisions but also because the product management process involves a lot of technical skills.

There are certain metrics that an enterprise will use to evaluate their products. These metrics might include the following:

> **Revenue or profit**: A good product is one which generates a lot of money for the company.

Customer satisfaction: A good product will get good reviews and a high rating. This will lead to more customers being satisfied with your product, leading to higher sales. However, if you make the wrong decisions, you might end up losing customers instead of gaining them because it is hard to please everybody.

Number of users: If a product becomes very popular, you can have lots of customers who are using it. It will also lead to a high amount of revenue.

Product acceptance: A good product will be widely accepted by the people as well as the company itself. The company will decide to invest more money into it, which will allow for better research and development. In addition, you will be able to launch new products down the road with ease because you already have a good reputation behind you, making things even easier.

Time to market: This is a metric that indicates how long it would have taken for a product to be developed and launched if the time was not spent on product management.

Number of new products launched: A good product will lead to lots of products being launched, even if they are not very successful. When you launch too many products, you can lose focus, which in turn will lead to less revenues. You might also be able to gain more attention from your competitors.

Time to success: This is a metric that indicates how long it would have taken for a product to be successful if the time was not spent on product management.

Time to failure: This metric indicates how long it would have taken for a product to fail if the time was not spent on product management.

In order to truly understand how well a product is doing, you need to take into consideration different factors such as the following:

The target market for the product: A good product will have a good target market that is easy to reach. The smaller the market, the more expensive the production. You can decide to make your products bigger in order to get better sales but in doing you create problems such as overcapacity, which will lower production and decrease profits.

The size of the market: The larger your market, the more you can charge for your product. However, if you are no longer considered a leader or have lost the battle to your competitors, it will be hard to get people to buy from you.

The competition for a product: You should do research on what other companies are doing in this industry. If your competitors are working on the same ideas as yours, you might end up selling less hair straighteners than shampoo.

The competition's reputation: If you try to keep up with your competitor, they might be better than you because they have been in the industry for a longer period of time. If your competitors are doing a good job, you end up copying their strategies instead of coming up with new ones.

The cost for a product: A good product can offer the same benefit as a high-priced product, but will still be able to sell at a cheaper price during the startup phase.

The profit for a product: A good product will make a lot of money for the company which in turn will make the company more successful. You can decide to lower your prices or add more features to your products in order to keep up with the competition, but this will end up costing you.

The risk involved: You should consider what could go wrong with each project. For example, if you are creating an item that does not have much experience and you do not know what it wants, it might be very difficult to sell.

In short: The product management process is difficult. It requires you to be comfortable with uncertainty, have a strong sense of creativity, meet an aggressive deadline, and have excellent communication skills. You need to make the right choices when it comes to perceiving market research information and technical data, which can be very challenging at times. You will also need to work hard in order to understand the needs of your customers instead of making assumptions about them.

4.3 Journey of an IoT Product

IoT products are the next frontier in technology. It has opened up a world of possibilities to create devices that can communicate with each other, work together, and help make your life easier. It is clear that many companies are betting on the IoT market to be the next big thing.

But developing IoT products is not as easy as it looks. There are several factors that one needs to take into consideration when designing an IoT product, which will be discussed in detail in this chapter along with some useful resources.

What Is the IoT Product Companies' Point of View

IoT products are the next frontier in technology. It has opened up a world of possibilities to create devices that can communicate with each other, work together, and help make your life easier.

- The IT industry and IoT device development research are ongoing.

- IoT product development market is growing rapidly.

- Businesses are evolving with the help of the IoT product development stage so they can explore their opportunities in the rapidly changing world of devices, connectivity, and digital services.

- Connected devices can be used for delivering a wide range of business values.

- IoT product development is an integral part of the digital transformation journey, and device manufacturers are quickly realizing that to create a successful connected device, they need to bring in the proper product owners, designers, software developers, and data scientists together to build a complete product.

– IoT product development is embodied into the foundation of every modern organization's digital transformation strategy.

– Top IoT product development companies include Microsoft, IBM, and GE.

– Estimation of the market is done from $15.7 billion in 2022 to reach more than $70 billion by 2025.

– By 2025, the market is expected to reach nearly $192 billion.

The IoT product development process involves a wide range of skills such as software development, hardware design, communication design, and cloud computing services.

What Is the IoT Product Consumers' Point of View

IoT products are the next big thing in consumer electronics. From smart TVs to smart home appliances, to wearables, and more, IoT products offer consumers the potential to interact with and control their personal devices in a new way.

– IoT products are not just limited to hardware. If a particular product can connect to your phone, it's likely an IoT product.

– Research is going on in smart home product development.

– Smart home market is growing rapidly.

- Businesses are evolving with the help of the IoT product development stage so they can explore their opportunities in the rapidly changing world of devices, connectivity, and digital services.

- IoT product development services many business verticals.

- Connected devices can be used for delivering a wide range of business values.

- IoT product development is an integral part of the digital transformation journey, and device manufacturers are quickly realizing that to create a successful connected device, they need to bring in the proper product owners, designers, software developers, and data scientists together to build a complete product.

- IoT product development is embodied into the foundation of every modern organization's digital transformation strategy.

- Top IoT product development companies include Microsoft, IBM, and GE.

- Estimation of the market is done from $11.

How to Develop an IoT Product from Scratch

IoT product development is a challenging and complicated process. However, if you are looking to build a product that's going to make you rich in the future, then developing an innovative IoT product might be just what you need.

- Determining the market size of IoT products

- Determining the success criteria of your IoT products

- Selecting the right team for developing your product

- Selecting a good enough technology for building an IoT product

- Selecting the best manufacturing partners for your products

- Selecting the best way to market the product

- Making a prototype of your product (if you want to build it yourself)

So now that we have gathered what the IoT is and how companies and consumers are looking at its development, let's discuss some ways in which we can develop an IoT product from scratch:

- If you want to develop an IoT product, it is important to decide whether you would like to develop your own product or find someone to help you with the development.

- If you are thinking of developing your own IoT product and have not done so already, then you will need to start with a basic understanding of data science and hardware design.

- If you already have a development team in place, then it would be best if they understand the basics of IoT products.

Main Considerations Before Developing an IoT Product

There are multiple factors that need to be thought over when developing an IoT product.

- Consumers will be the first ones to try out your product, so make sure that you have a good idea about how your product should look like and what it should do.

- Also keep in mind not only the functionality of your IoT product but also its look as well as branding and marketing. The design of any device is extremely important, as it will be one of its biggest selling points.

- Product development has become increasingly complex today. This is because the products that are being used have become more and more advanced in the recent times.

- There are many of things that need to be taken care of before you finalize the development of any product.

- If you want to develop an IoT product for a particular industry, you should research about the industries and decide whether it is something that interests your company.

- Once you have decided what your product will do, then you should focus on how your product will work as well as how it will be marketed.

- You will also need to think about the overall look of your device and its features that will set it apart from other products.

- You should also consider appointing a team to come up with the best possible design for your product.

- Once you have finalized all these points, you can start with the development.

Difference Between IoT Product Development Different from Conventional Devices

The new generation of IoT products are very different from conventional devices in many ways.

- Although the primary purpose of any device is to provide functionality, IoT products must also provide an experience of their own.

- If you are thinking about developing a conventional device, then you should remember that you will need a team of hardware and software engineers who will be responsible for the development.

- However, in the case of IoT products, it is important to have a team with skills in data science and software designing as well as communication and cloud services designing.

- If you are planning to make your own IoT device, then it is recommended that you have the skills to design hardware as well as the ability to work on embedded software.

- It is important for the type of presentation of an IoT product to be appealing and attractive to the user. This also goes for factors like website and IoT apps development.

- One of the biggest challenges in developing an IoT device is that a lot of time and effort needs to go into testing your product.

- It is important to have a team that can take the necessary steps in testing your IoT device for its compatibility.

- Also, it is important to make sure that your product does not have any bugs and that it is adequately tested before being brought on the market.

There are various ways in which an IoT device can be developed.

- There are two main types of development – embedded and cloud based.

- Cloud-based method of IoT product development is the one which requires a great deal of expertise, as compared to embedded device development. However, it is the most common way for many companies.

- If you develop a good IoT product, then it will be good for business and will help your company in making a profit.

- For developing an IoT device in cloud-based method, there are certain things that need to be kept in mind.

- You will need to have a good enough amount of cloud infrastructure and connectivity so that your product can operate smoothly.

- There are also very few choices for cloud-based IoT solutions, and the one that you choose should be compatible with your IoT device.

- If you choose an incorrect solution, then it could lead to a variety of problems for your product.

- The development cost of any cloud-based IoT solution is very high, and you will need a significant amount of investment for this purpose.

IoT Hardware vs. Software for Development

IoT hardware is used for developing an IoT device, because it includes all the components that are needed to support and maintain your product.

- However, your IoT software could be developed in two ways – cloud based or embedded.

–   If you have decided to develop your own device using embedded software, then you will need a team of software engineers as well as hardware engineers.

–   Embedded development is more expensive than the cloud-based one and if done incorrectly can lead to a number of problems for your product.

–   If you choose to go with embedded software for your product, then make sure that you have a good enough budget for the project.

–   Cloud IoT development is more flexible and provides more freedom to the user than embedded software.

–   Cloud-based IoT development is also very affordable and is easily affordable by most companies.

–   If you choose to go with cloud-based IoT software, then there are certain things that need to be kept in mind while making your choice.

–   You will need to make sure that the solution you choose is compatible with your product and also that it is cloud based.

–   The best way of looking at cloud IoT development for any company is to research about the best cloud-based solutions for a particular industry.

–   You will need to make sure that the solution that you have chosen meets all the requirements and has all the features that your product will require. You should also consider a variety of other factors while looking at cloud-based solutions.

- It is also important to remember that cloud-based IoT development requires a high level of expertise.

- Even small mistakes can lead to a huge loss for your company, and hence you should be very careful while choosing the solution for your product.

- If you want to develop an IoT device, then it is recommended that you have the skills to design hardware as well as the ability to work on embedded software.

- You should also consider appointing a team to make sure that your product meets all the standards and requirements.

- Once you have finalized all these points, you can start with the development.

What Are the Business Risks of IoT

If done incorrectly or if done by a person who does not have adequate knowledge about developing an IoT product, then it can lead to a number of problems for your company.

- If you develop an IoT device for business, then it is important that it meets all the standards and requirements of your organization.

- If you go with a style of development in which the business needs to pay more than the initial investment, then this will also lead to more problems for your company.

- There are many places where an IoT device can fail or fail easily, which leads to very high losses for a company in case they do not have proper plans in place.

- If there are too many IoT devices on the market, then customers will not be able to figure out which one is best.

- There are also other factors that lead to problems with customer experience, like customer service and app enhancement, apart from the way in which your product is designed.

- Even if you are providing a good customer experience for your customer, but if you have faulty products, it will also lead to a loss for your company.

- There are various ways in which the risk of your product is reduced if you do not take adequate steps in reducing this risk.

- If you want to develop an IoT device, then it is important that you keep your eye on all the risks involved with developing your product.

- You should make sure that you choose a team of experts who know how to develop IoT devices in a way that they are compatible with all the aspects required by your company.

- If your product has a variety of different parts, then you should make sure that they are compatible with each other.

- Even developing internal infrastructure should be given attention to.

- When you have a product in place, it is important that you start taking the necessary steps to reduce the risk of failure or any other problem faced by your company.

- The best way of doing this is by making sure that your IoT device is developed in a way that it can easily be maintained and used by customers.

- There are several ways that you can make sure that your product is developed in a manner that it is compatible with all the business needs.

- It is also important to keep in mind the methods of handling and delivering your product, along with the costs involved.

- When you have devised a plan for your product, then it is important that you take adequate steps to reduce any risks involved.

- When you have ironed out the plan for your product and you are ready to start with the development, then it is important that you hire a team of experts who will make sure that all the components are compatible with each other.

- This is a very important step and should be given utmost importance.

- There are also many benefits of working with a team of experts, as they are more likely to develop an IoT device that works without any issues.

CHAPTER 5

IoT Product Manager and Life Cycle Management

Product management is one of the most demanding jobs in software. It requires an intense balance between creativity, business knowledge, detail orientation, and leadership skills. This template will serve as a guide to help you land your first product management job.

Product management is the set of activities and skills needed to bring a product from inception to launch. Product managers are responsible for defining, selling, developing, and managing the products that they make. At the top of product management is a manager who has the responsibility to define, sell, and manage projects through their entirety. This manager typically represents an executive in charge of software development or marketing. Product managers are often external consultants who work on behalf of companies with strong business needs or internal employees who help market and develop software developed by their department.

Product management is a great job for many because it offers a variety of skills that can be utilized in many different fields. Students on the technical side can use their ability to analyze and understand technology in order to develop products, while students on the business side can utilize their understanding of business processes and customer needs to develop superior products.

© Padmaraj Nidagundi 2022
P. Nidagundi, *The IoT Product Manager*, https://doi.org/10.1007/978-1-4842-8631-9_5

However, becoming a product manager is not an easy task. While there are some companies who appreciate work experience, most companies favor candidates with an advanced degree. Most job candidates in product management are holding degrees in business administration, marketing, and engineering. Since these degrees take anywhere from three to six years to complete, most people who hold them are already employed full time.

If you are still interested in product management, here are some tips to help you get started:

Understand your business needs: Product managers need to have a thorough understanding of the field they work with. You should understand what kind of customers you serve, their needs, and how your product can satisfy these needs.

Shape the future: Product managers should be responsible for shaping the future of their product. They should be responsible for determining what will happen with their product and who will be using it.

Overcome obstacles: Product managers need to understand challenges and have experience working through them. While product management does not normally include obstacles, you should know how to work around the most common ones. For instance, you do not want your products to fail because of a lack of understanding of the market or a lack of trust between a customer and a vendor. If a problem does present itself, you should be able to work around it and still meet your goal.

Business acumen: You need to understand how business works. You should know what costs are associated with developing a product, how these costs are accrued, and who incurs them. You also need to know when you can charge for a product and when you cannot. In addition, you need to have an understanding of the products on the market today and how they affect your product.

Make decisions: Product managers are in charge of making decisions with business implications. They should be able to make swift and informed decisions to ensure their product's success.

Communicate effectively: Product managers need to be able to communicate effectively with both internal and external groups. They should know not only the technical side of the business but also how to speak in a way that speaks directly to others. Communication is critical for product development since you have limited time and resources when developing a new product.

Keep up with technology: Product managers should be able to stay up to date with technology. The market is changing as quickly as new products are being introduced, and you will have limited time to understand and adapt. As time progresses, you will need to be just as quick at adapting.

Be flexible: Product managers need to be mentally flexible in order to work well in a rapidly changing environment. Just because a product has worked successfully for others does not mean it will work for you. Every product is different, and you will have to take your customer's needs into account before creating a new product.

5.1 IoT PM Conducts a Research

With the advent of the Internet of Things, you can now research your product and make guesses about where it is going. You will build a prototype, expand on its features, and create a sales pitch for it that would make an Olympic-level swimmer blush at the money you've made.

That's why we hired a product manager with their own in-house research department.

You have: A master's degree in computer science specializing in artificial intelligence, neurobiology, or similar. You love life and believe a robot can never replace you. You've based your entire existence on this fact. A proven track record of creating features and products for the Internet of Things market for companies like Apple, Google, and Hewlett-Packard. A portfolio of patents on various aspects of product development as applied to consumer electronics. You have a unique relationship with your wife. Ninety-nine percent of the time she thinks you're awesome, but that remaining 1% of the time you worry she's getting tired of you and will leave you for someone less needy.

Deals with: Creating models and metrics to assess market penetration in the IoT sector. Creating various scenarios to predict the development of future products, which will then be used in our sales pitch at Strategy Day. Leading research into various aspects of the Internet of Things such as its impact on our lives and how it will ultimately evolve into a full-fledged society.

Research to developing the real product: Trying to develop a new product or business? You're the Internet of Things manager; you take pride in your ability to research and develop new product ideas. But if all it takes is a few hours researching, you can easily be spending weeks or even months developing an idea that turns out to be a dud. So how can you avoid wasting your time and effort?

I was on a panel at the recent (and stellar) "Thinking Conference" in Toronto, and we spent a couple hours discussing what makes good product managers. I ended up spending some time talking about how to research an upcoming product idea, and it really struck a chord with some of the other panelists who were new to the space. The process was the same for all of us: you put together a couple of PMs and execute a research session to discover if an idea is worth pursuing.

From my experience, the key to finding value in this research is asking better questions. The most important decision you will make when researching your product or business is how much time and effort to put into it. Are you going to use your free time or dedicate your Monday to the best effort? Are you going to hire a firm to do the work for you?

All depends on how valuable that research is. Here's how I decide.

First, you have to define your project. I'll use a startup as an example: it's nothing but a technology. You don't have a product or service, so any idea that falls under this category isn't going to be very valuable – even if the technology is great and could become one of the best products in the world. But it's still useless research unless you know why it's useless.

You have to define your research.

How big is your market? If it's huge, and the product is a hit, then the research is valuable. If it's small, then the research isn't worth much. In our case, we are targeting tens of millions of users with very expensive installed bases; we better believe that our product will be valuable. What alternative options do you have in the space? Novelty and innovation may drive some segmentation and differentiation while driving down costs. If your competitors are all known quantities, then you will have to work harder to make your value proposition special. In our case, there are a number of vendors for which the cost of entry is hundreds of thousands or millions of dollars; this eliminates the majority of our competition. On the other hand, if you can obtain a monopoly position in the market because your product is superior, then that's an incredibly valuable position to be in.

But will you be able to do this? How much venture capital is required to get a foothold in the market? If you don't have VCs in your corner, this is going to be extremely limiting. If you have all the money in the world, it's a little better. A niche business model can be done but requires a lot more resources. In our case, we were able to get a $2.5 million investment, which was enough to get a working proof of concept but not enough to scale the product widely.

How long will it take you to develop? I've seen people spend five years developing a product, and then the technology changes and their product becomes obsolete before they even launch. In our case, it's more like three years to get something working, and then another six to nine months of fine tuning after launch. And it's not just about scope but about doing things right the first time. To my mind, there is no excuse for creating a crappy product that is half-baked from the start. Are you willing to change your idea? It's always an opportunity cost.

Once you're done with your research, you should have a pretty good idea of the answer to the question: how much is it worth to me? If it's not too hard, and there's some value, then you can create a pretty credible plan for execution.

I talked about software development, but this can apply to any kind of research.

How to present your research as a PM?

Just take an example. You are a product manager for the Internet of Things (IoT). You have been tasked with creating a software dashboard which will allow your company to better manage and automate their product offerings. Once you have drafted the dashboard, you have to decide on the most effective way to present your data.

The data is collected from the IoT devices through an API in JSON format. The data is converted to a CSV file and will be presented on a visual dashboard. The dashboard will have a clean interface, with lime green and white being the most prominent colors.

For the product summary, you need to present:

This should include how many of each product have been ordered on average over the last year and how much each device costs for maintenance per year.

For the main dashboard, you need to present:

This should include how much each device costs for maintenance per year. The value of these numbers is different depending on what kind of device and what maintenance plan was purchased.

The data is collected from the IoT devices through an API in JSON format. The data is converted to a CSV file and will be presented on a visual dashboard. The dashboard will have a clean interface, with lime green and white being the most prominent colors.

This should include

1. The number of products that were sold over the last year.

2. The increase in sales since the previous year (negative if the product was discontinued),

3. The number of units that are in the distribution center and how many have been sold over the last week.

4. The number of units that are in the customer's home (or business) and in service for a given period of time for each month, along with the total number of devices available during each period.

5. Numbers for each of the customers we are tracking, including total sales, number of units that are in service, and price of services.

6. This should include how much money was spent on services from each customer per month.

7. This should include how many new customers we have on average each month and how many contacts we have from each customer per month. We also need to know if any of the customers has ordered more products than the average over the last year.

8. This should include how long it takes to ship a device from the warehouse and how long it takes to get it installed in the customer's home or business.

9. This should include how many devices we have purchased and how much each device costs.

10. This should include any other information you want to add.

You have presented your product and the visual summary in a presentation and the requirements for making it are clearly defined. In this case, we have a clear product summary (Product Name, Link to Product Description) which is highlighted in lime green; there is also a list of FAQs to present as well. The information that is shown on each page should be clearly defined. These are also limited to two pages and can be displayed on a single page if needed.

5.1.1 IoT Development vs. Software Development

The new emerging industry of the Internet of Things is developing at an exponential rate. IoT technology has enabled the connection of any number of devices to networks and obtaining data from them, as well as having a say in what those devices do. Over the past couple years, many people have been researching the benefits that IoT-integrated systems could potentially bring to a wide range of industries including healthcare, transportation, and energy.

The problem with the IoT technology is that it has the potential to include millions of devices and these devices will need to be managed. Therefore, software developers are being asked to develop software applications for this technology. But since there are so many devices connected through a single platform, we will need to write more software.

This means an increase in the amount of program code and system capabilities needed for operation and maintenance. The exponential growth of IoT applications is driving software development standards and maintenance needs.

So, which comes first into one's mind – the IoT or the software? For a software developer, the answer is "Both!" The software developer must first create and design an IoT system, as well as develop code for it. The code that is written will depend on what type of application is being developed. Then, the software developer must create applications to monitor and control the IoT system.

In this chapter, I will discuss the differences between IoT development and software development.

IoT Software Development

The IoT is the Internet's newest buzzword; it's currently being used for a multitude of hardware systems, from light bulbs to connected cars to home automation devices such as thermostats and switches. The term IoT is being used for a wide range of devices since everyone is trying to hook up their digital devices.

On the other hand, software development has been around for decades. Since then, many vendors and developers have created all sorts of software for different use cases across many industries. Generally speaking, software development can be categorized into three categories:

> **Application development**: This is the process of creating an application from scratch using development languages such as Java, C++, PHP, etc.
>
> **Systems development**: This is the process of creating an application that can run on a particular operating system and also create executable files (object code) and libraries (source code) with which to build other applications.
>
> **Integration**: The process of integrating the developed software components throughout the application, as well as making sure that all of the existing software components work together properly.

For an IoT developer to create systems for smart devices, he or she needs to have a significant knowledge in the area of systems development. But IoT systems are more complex than normal systems, since they involve devices that can talk to one another over a network. All of the devices must be connected together, securely and reliably.

IoT development requires a software developer to have a deeper knowledge of the protocols involved. For example, Zigbee is one of the many communication protocols being used for communicating with sensors over short distances. This protocol is used to ensure that data sent from these sensors is protected and accurate when sent across an Internet-connected network.

IoT Development vs. Software Development

In short, software developers are essentially the backbone of the IoT industry, since IoT is disseminated almost entirely through technology. So, if you are looking to work on something cutting edge, consider getting into IoT development or software development. Both fields seem promising for developers at this point in time. As always, you must consider a couple factors before deciding on whether to get into these areas – mainly your own capabilities and what opportunities are currently available.

5.1.2 IoT PM Focuses on Team Management

Product managers are the link between strategy and execution. Day to day, they're in charge of product development and delivery.

More than just a project manager, product managers need to be able to deliver results with an understanding of both user experience and business goals. A successful product manager needs to be technically savvy, understand metrics and data analysis methods, have domain expertise in the space they're targeting for growth, and more than anything else: they need empathy. Product managers are responsible for the "big picture" of the product, but they also have to stay in control of all the different aspects that make up a great product.

Here are some tips and tricks on managing a team of developers to get more done and keep them happy and on track.

A good product manager needs to be able to carry out the vision that's set for them in an actionable way, taking into consideration each step along the way and ensuring that it is executed as best it can be.

The easiest way to keep a team on track is to delegate and prioritize tasks. Make sure that you are delegating all of the tasks that need to be done each week, along with any subtasks that need to be completed, and make sure that you are communicating this clearly to your team.

> *Good project management, good organization, defines depen-dencies and leaves no room for ambiguity.*
>
> —Steve Blank

Product managers need to be able to manage their time efficiently and rely on the help of their engineering background. You need to set clear timelines for your team so that they have a benchmark they can use to see success or failure at regular intervals, without any ambiguity. This will help keep them motivated and productive.

IOT TEAM MANAGEMENT

Take care of your product (your internal and external stakeholders) so that it is always functioning to its best potential for the whole company.

> *If we lose focus in our priorities, we lose the overall vision, and we start making mistakes.*
>
> —Kevin Kelly

Keeping an open line of communication is essential for a successful team from day one. Make sure to set up regular meetings to check in with your team, or a single meeting to go through the milestones of each project that you have given out. This will help maintain clear direction and keep everyone on the same page.

Listed in the following are some of the best tools that can help product managers manage teams effectively:

> **Trello**: Trello is a popular tool for those who are looking for a team management platform that's free and easy to use. Trello allows you to organize projects into boards and cards and manages your tasks in lists through drag-and-drop. Your team can set due dates and add labels alongside every task they complete.

> **Asana**: Asana is another project management software that is great for organizing and communicating with teams. While Asana is a paid tool, you can try it out for free if you use a computer or mobile device for six months.

> **Mattermost product management tools**: Mattermost product management is essential for organizations, and there are dozens of tools designed specifically for managing teams. The Mattermost team management page allows you to set priorities, assign tasks to your team members, monitor their progress, and add feedback on the status of each project from the team members themselves.

These are some of the best tools that product managers can use to help organize their team, keep track of the different tasks for each project, and add feedback on the status of the projects.

The following are some of the ways to create a collaborative environment:

> **Establish trust**: Being transparent and open is essential for building a product team. It will get your team members to trust you more and helps them understand your vision. The trust you get through transparency will help build the culture of your organization.

> **Delegate tasks**: If you are a lone wolf, it may not be the best approach to managing a team, especially if they work in different time zones or need an expert level of knowledge to complete a task. So, always try to consider your team toggling tasks and responsibilities so that you can delegate the work to them.

> **Be open and honest with your team**: This is key for building trust. Be open with them about the tasks you want them to complete, share your plans and decisions with them, ask questions, and listen to their feedback. It's the best way to keep them informed and on track.

> **Discuss openly**: When it comes to discussing issues regarding a project, being open is important as well. So, trying to discuss about the work in a closed-off manner may not be the best approach. Instead, try to discuss openly and share your ideas on how it should get executed.

Manage likes and dislikes: This is a great way to realize if there are any issues regarding a particular feature or product that you are developing. Try to involve all of your team members in discussing different aspects of the product that they feel they need or don't want. It will help you realize their problems or concerns about the product and you can work out on a solution.

The primary objective of a Product Manager is to deliver a world-class product that delights its users.

—Diane Greene

There are different types of product managers out there, and no two roles are alike. Some businesses need to be agile and innovative, while others need to be more traditional in execution.

The most common type of product manager is the traditional product manager, who follows a set of predetermined guidelines. They are great at understanding the product requirements and coming up with a solution that is easy and quick to implement. The straightforward working style also helps them get along well with the other staff members in the organization.

As soon as Product Management teams start to achieve critical mass, they become agents for change as much as they can actually design and implement change.

—Jeff Gothelf

The goal of the DevOps product manager is to take a software development life cycle (SDLC) and implement it in the company's development process. They are known for their creative approach to product management and are typically young, creative, and individualistic.

This type of product manager is great at bringing new ideas into the picture and sticking with them until they are implemented. They tend to work better in teams as they thrive on acting as a catalyst for change within organizations.

5.1.3 IoT PM Focuses on Product Strategic Decisions

If you're a product manager and you're looking for ways to make better decisions, let's talk about how you can do it. Understanding the difference between tactical and strategic decisions as well as their associated process is key to making better decisions because those will depend on your company's strategy. So if this is your first time reading our chapter, we'll walk through how these work so that you can use that information to make better strategic decisions.

> *When I say "strategic decision", I mean an important decision that bears on the future of the company and its products.*
>
> —James Dixon

The first thing to do is to understand some of the differences between tactical decisions and strategic decisions. Tactical decisions are those that are made in real time by people working on a product. In contrast, strategic decisions are made after a product has been created. Clearly, strategic decisions are made at the product management level of an organization.

How to make a product strategic decision?

The interesting thing about strategic decisions is that they have an effect on the future of a product. Usually, those decisions are made by senior management, and they are very important to the company. Sometimes, they create the vision of the company in terms of what it will offer its customers.

Examples of strategic decision making: It could be a decision to acquire another company which is done by senior management in order to create a new product (making it more competitive). On the other hand, it could be a decision to eliminate a product or service that is not growing well. Or it might be a decision to create a new product line of services. Once those decisions are made, the company will focus on promoting them and making sure that they become successful.

A product manager in charge of making strategic decisions: A good product manager will understand what are the best strategic decisions for his organization, and he'll make sure that they are implemented successfully. They are responsible for finding out the best products and services to add to the company's portfolio. It is critical for a PM that they have a good understanding of what is happening in the market to make their decisions. They also have to have a strong vision for the future and be able to communicate it really well. They need to be able to prioritize their projects and allocate them in order for them all to succeed.

IOT PRODUCT
STRATEGIC DECISIONS

How do you make a tactical decision?

At the tactical level, decisions are made by product management teams. They are the ones who make prototype designs, physical parts, and software. This is how a product is formed. The teams are responsible for making sure that the product meets their design specifications and that it is well made. The job of the product manager in charge of tactical decisions is to help their team with these things.

Other responsibilities include managing time, resources, and meetings organized by product managers in order to devote uninterrupted time to their projects while they focus on getting the best out of it.

Examples of tactical decision making: It could be a decision to change the design of a product because of feedback from customers. It could be a decision to move forward with the development of a product even though it is missing some details that were not thought out initially. Or it might be a decision to cancel an idea and start over because it will take too much time or money to make it happen. These are all tactical decisions that you might come across as you work as a product manager and they happen in real time.

Tactical decisions will happen as you work on your products and they can often change based on feedback that you get. For example, a customer might tell you that they don't like something about the product and this can make you change it. That's why decision making, especially at the tactical level, is very important for all product managers.

A product manager in charge of making tactical decisions: While these decisions are made by a product management team, the PM in charge of making tactical decisions will be the one who will manage the whole process. They will work on how to get teams together and how to keep them motivated during the production process. They must also make sure that they have a clear understanding on what is going on in their teams to make better strategic decisions.

Working at the tactical level is not unlike working with a software product. You will have to make changes, test it, and repeat these steps to make sure that your product is well received in the market. In short, being a PM at this level will give you an opportunity to gain experience and learn how to manage your time. It's great experience for aspiring PMs because there is always something new happening in the world of technology.

5.1.4 IoT PM Focuses on Better Time Management Structures

Time management is an important skill to have as a product manager. It can be difficult to focus on your tasks without being able to manage small windows of time between them. This chapter offers some tips on how time management can help product managers in the workplace.

One way many people find success at managing their schedules is by using a time structure, or a schedule that breaks your day into manageable blocks with designated times for doing different types of work. These blocks are usually set in terms of a specific amount of time, like 15 minutes, and may be set to arise based on the time of day.

Product managers can benefit from "time blocking" but need to adjust their own schedule to the demands they are putting on it. A key point is understanding how much time you actually have and critical "resource" moments where more than likely you will take a break. Time blocking lets you block out these moments in advance and can also be a good way to define your focus for the day.

Tips for effective time management:

#1: Automate time management (if you can)

It's always been very helpful for me to automate any part of my schedule such as diary notifications, reminders, and so on. This is because the tasks I'm trying to complete are usually time sensitive and I have limited mental capacity to remember what I need to do.

#2: Focus on getting stuff done, not just busyness

As a product manager, you should be aiming for effectiveness at doing the right things, not just getting lots of things done. It's important to prioritize what tasks are really important and give them the necessary time to be completed.

#3: Avoid distractions

Your smartphone and other sources of distraction can quickly derail your focus; so if you really want to get a task completed, shut them off!

#4: Practice good time management habits at work and home

As well as defining your tasks, it's also useful to define when you will do them.

#5: Learn to say no

If you say yes to everything and anything, then you're probably not being effective in your day-to-day tasks.

#6: Find a mentor

Discuss your time management and coaching with others; this helps to keep you accountable.

#7: Outsource time management tasks

If you're struggling to get your head around planning your days, ask someone else to do it for you.

#8: Use project management software

Use project management software such as Asana or Microsoft Project. Here, you can save ideas and sort them out by due date or priority, which can be a useful way of straightening out any work overload.

#9: Set realistic deadlines and stick to them

For any task you want to finish, set a deadline for it and stick to it. If you're having trouble getting this, check that your goal is realistic – don't be tempted to add in extra hours.

#10: Use templates for recurring tasks

If you have any recurring tasks such as technical or design work, try and set up templates you can use with ease over and over again.

How to improve productivity with better time management?

Time management charts are a really good way to show productivity in your daily work.

Time management charts also allow you to easily see what tasks and projects are taking up more time than others. This helps with making better use of your time and focus on the areas that need improvement or that have been neglected.

Tips for working with time management charts:

1. If time management is new to you, start small. At first, try creating a chart of one day, and then gradually increase it to a week or a month.

2. Make your time management chart at the same time every day.

3. Use the same format for your time management chart every time you make it. If you have to fill in a lot of information, you're more likely to forget about it and/or skip some tasks, which may hurt your productivity.

4. Make sure you include all important tasks on your time management chart so that nothing gets left out that should be included.

5. Since time management is such a crucial part of your daily productivity, consider printing out a copy of your chart and making it available at work.

This is one of the greatest time management tools for product managers. A time tracking app can not only help you to keep track of how much time you spend working on specific tasks but also add up all your hours worked during the day, week, and month. There are many good products out there.

How to improve time management?

1. Create a resource plan to follow a certain procedure and spend time wisely.

2. Prioritize important tasks and plan them first in your daily schedule. These tasks should be completed as soon as possible which can help you avoid procrastination and deadlines.

3. Get rid of distractions by blocking out the time you want to focus.

4. Make sure you allocate enough time on your tasks that require more preparation and collecting data.

5. Recognize and avoid bad habits or negative thoughts that could distract you from your work.

5.2 Managing a Product Backlog

The IoT (Internet of Things) is the next stage of the Internet evolution. With the IoT, you'll finally be able to collect data from all your home appliances, fixtures, and other things around the house. That's why it's important for product backlog management to be a priority in your IoT business strategy.

This chapter I discussed about an example of Nest thermostat company and how they work on product backlog management.

Many IoT devices are connected to the Internet already, but still have limited functionality. For example, your home alarm system at home is now connected to the Internet, allowing you to control it remotely through your smartphone. But there still isn't much you can do with it. You go into the app and change a few settings here and there, but it doesn't do much more than that.

What I've noticed is that the most advanced IoT devices are those with features that allow people to create new and innovative use cases.

This is where product backlog management comes into the picture. A great example of this is Nest's smart thermostat, which uses product backlog management to create an ecosystem of sensors, apps, and other devices that can be integrated into your home.

The Nest thermostat works with the following features: The first is Farsight, which lets Nest interact with other devices in your home that are activated by heat, light, or motion. In other words, it will know when you're home or not and adjust the temperature accordingly. The second feature is called Away Assist, which detects if you've left home. When it does this, it shuts down all the devices you've set to turn off while away. The third feature is Auto-Away, which takes note of when you're not at home and programs your thermostat to automate some energy-saving features.

As you can see, Nest's thermostat is an intelligent device that does a lot more than just heat up and cool down the room. It's also a part of a larger ecosystem that lets people use their home devices in ways they couldn't before.

Product backlog management for IoT devices is about getting a clearer picture of the set of features your IoT device needs to have. And by giving it more capabilities, you can create a more impactful product.

The best thing about this type of product backlog management is that you don't need to know exactly what it will look like. You just need to know what the core features are and then define a clear set of use cases around them.

But what are some of these features?

Well, there are several features that you should consider as a product owner and product manager for an IoT device. These include the following:

Sensors: Sensor will collect data about the user's location and environment. For example, there are wireless sensors that you can install in your house to track humidity, temperature, and other environmental factors that affect the indoor climate.

Configurable sensors: Sensors are one thing, but they can't do much without some kind of logic to make use of them. For example, your smart light bulb can use the weather information it receives to automatically turn on and off. You add just a little logic to the sensor to make use of it.

Highly cooperative sensors: Speaking of sensors, you can also add sensors that integrate with you and other devices without needing much configuration. For example, there are wireless sensor modules that can connect to a cloud service over the Internet and send the information in real time.

Hardware: Hardware features include things like the device's display, controller, and sensors. For example, a smart thermostat might have a display that shows the current temperature inside the room. You can also connect other devices to it like an air conditioner or humidifier (through a wireless relay).

Software: Software features include software that runs the device. For example, some apps let you change the temperature on the thermostat by simply clicking on a symbol or other interface element displayed on the display of your thermostat.

Product feature: One of the most important and probably the hardest to define feature is the product feature. This is the most important feature that the company should focus on while building the product. Product features are usually product related, but sometimes they can be outside of the product, like a service or something else. For example, a smart thermostat might include an app that aggregates all data collected by your thermostat and sends it to another cloud service over the Internet where it can be used by other people or companies.

IoT device monitoring: The device monitoring and management feature lets you manage your IoT device from anywhere you have Internet access. This lets you monitor the device's condition, like the current battery status or the capacity of its integrated storage. You can even use this feature for troubleshooting purposes since you can see if any of the devices that your IoT device is connected to are malfunctioning. The thing about monitoring and managing IoT devices is that it's something every company should be doing already.

IoT data collection and visualization: This feature lets people (including you) collect data from IoT devices and visualize it in various ways. There are numerous ways to visualize the data collected by IoT devices. For example, a smart thermostat could use a standard calendar view to show the current temperature inside your house on a particular day. You can also use the same data to generate statistics about the indoor climate over multiple days or even weeks and months.

How to do the product backlog prioritization?

Now that you know what you can include on your product road map, it's time to figure out what should be prioritized first. One way to do this is to decide on a set of three small features that your IoT device needs and then prioritize them afterward.

You might have also realized by now that you could do quite a few things with your IoT product. The best thing about this kind of product backlog management is that you don't have to think of everything at once if it's too overwhelming. For example, you could start with one sensor and then work your way up from there.

What's the best way to prioritize the product backlog?

There are different ways to prioritize each requirement on your product backlog, but you probably only need one for this kind of product. A popular method is called the MoSCoW method which stands for these four options: must have, should have, could have, won't fix.

Must-have features are the most important ones that you need to implement for your product. If you miss a must-have feature, your product might not be successful in the market. Don't forget that even if there are several must-have requirements on your list, you shouldn't work on them all at once because the project wouldn't have any focus if you do. Pick a few of them and implement them one by one.

Should-have features are things that you need, but they might not be that important, or they will work better if they are implemented later.

Could-have features need to be added to the product, but it's doubtful whether they will help you achieve your goal. For example, it's good to include a wireless sensor module on your product, but the sensor might not really give you the desired data.

5.3 How an IoT PM Engages with Stakeholders to Scope Work

The product manager is the go-to person for stakeholders and the project sponsor, so it is important to engage with them well. The product manager needs to outline what work will happen and when, so they need to identify what will be delivered, how it will be delivered, and who will do the work. They should keep their stakeholders informed about progress and solicit feedback as needed (e.g., via Agile retrospectives).

The product manager needs to document the requirements from their stakeholders, including the priority of delivery, risks, and what they are trying to achieve. They should also keep a log of requirements changes so they can check back if there is any ambiguity later.

Ensure that all work items are aligned with stakeholders' priorities and have a shared understanding of the scope of work and progress via status meetings, backlog grooming sessions, sprint reviews, and other tools. Status meetings should be held on regular schedule. They should be brief and regular, ideally held daily or every other day.

In Scrum, the product manager is embedded in the development team. This gives them more insight on what work needs to be done, so they can have a shared understanding with their teams of what backlog items will be delivered. By working closely with their teams (e.g., during daily Scrum meetings), product managers can ensure that everyone is on the same page and can make trade-offs or adjustments as needed.

Tips for IoT product manager: Product managers should ensure they have a clear understanding of the end user's needs, which includes the total cost of ownership and risk/benefit trade-offs associated with using IoT products. They must help prioritize requirements based on the goals of their organization, including timelines and budgets.

Product managers should also work with business analysts to understand the technical constraints for an IoT solution. This includes obtaining the right hardware, sensors, and any custom software. Product managers should ensure that it is well documented and understood by stakeholders.

Product managers should also ensure that any IoT solution has a feasible go-to-market strategy. For example, they might need to work with sales managers on pricing strategies while working with marketing teams on user education programs or integrating with existing platforms.

The product manager must also secure the needed resources for the project. This can include coordinating the work effort between different departments (e.g., hardware, software, software developers).

Product managers should also ensure that the development team follows project guidelines. This might include following check-ins or other practices.

Product managers can also be involved with meetings of additional stakeholders such as product marketing, sales, or legal teams to help coordinate the different parties. This can help manage the concept's life cycle and ensure that it stays fresh and up to date with requirements.

Product managers' and stakeholders' relation: Product managers can communicate effectively with stakeholders if they have an understanding of their needs. They need to understand their concerns and requirements. The key role of the product manager is to gather requirements from customers, gain stakeholder trust, and get buy-in before starting a project or releasing a new product. The product

manager should keep stakeholders informed about what is happening
in the company, so they can make decisions that will benefit them in the
long term.

5.4 How an IoT Product Manager Makes Critical Decisions

In the world of business, product managers typically wear many hats. They
might be in charge of managing the design and development process for a
product, or they could be tasked with planning out pricing and marketing
tactics. The truth is that these roles are just a few products that the product
manager might be responsible for across an organization. It can sometimes
feel overwhelming when you are expected to do so much at one time, but
there is no way around it if you expect to succeed as a product manager.

The product manager is the person responsible for ensuring that a
project comes in on time and within budget. In order to accomplish this,
they have to make a lot of tough decisions along the way. It is important
that a project is successful; however, it can be easy to fall into the trap of
taking one action over another just because it seems like it will be more
effective instead of following what your gut tells you. Here are some
effective ways for how a product manager can make critical decisions:

1. **Know your team's strengths**: Being able to understand your team's strengths is critical for the product manager. The fact that you have a great team dedicated to a project is the best proof that you made the right decision on the entire product. By creating a strong team, you are more likely to accomplish your goal than if you try and do it all by yourself.

2. **Use user research**: A lot of products are developed from market research conducted by focus groups and other similar efforts. However, it is important to remember that the end users are what really matter. If you want to make sure your entire project goes smoothly, then you need to compile all of your research data into one place and use it as a foundation for your decisions. User interviews and surveys provide the most effective way to do this.

3. **Be patient**: It can be difficult to wait for positive results after you make a big decision, but in many cases, it is necessary. For example, if you are developing a product and plan to release it in the near future, then you need to have patience. It can be easy to worry about what your competitors are doing, but that information may not be as important as your own current strategy.

4. **Knowing your competition is just as important**: It is important for the product manager to be aware of their competition's actions because it can influence how you decide to handle a project. For example, if a competitor releases a product that you were planning to develop, then you might want to change your plans in order to prevent being left behind.

5. **Balancing quality and profitability**: In many cases, the product manager can decide what to do by determining what will be the most profitable or effective for the organization. However, it is important not to lose sight of quality in order to ensure success.

6. **Think of the worst-case scenarios and how you would act on them**: It is important for the product manager to think about the worst scenarios that could occur. This will give them an idea of which direction they should take when making decisions, because they will be able to react quickly in order to prevent any significant damage from happening.

7. **Listen to your gut**: There is no way around it; sometimes you just have a feeling about whether or not something will work out like you want it to or not.

8. **Think about all the different stakeholders involved**, their needs and concerns, and how they might react to your decision or plan.

9. **Consider what is best for those who will be using your product.**

10. **Get the team involved in decision making, especially if it's their expertise you're relying on to deliver a successful end product**: Getting the whole team involved in decision making will ensure that everyone is aligned with the strategy and tasks that need to be accomplished in order to achieve success on the project.

Since there is no formula for creating a successful product manager, it is important that you stay learning and have a vision for what your goals are in the future. You can get more information on the various tools available that are great for those who are new to the industry. One final suggestion is to read about other product managers who have built successful products and learned how they executed on getting autonomy and freedom around their jobs. Just remember to always be yourself and be confident in your own abilities when it comes to making decisions.

5.5 How an IoT Product Manager Proposes Creative Solutions to Complex Problems

Many people think that IoT product managers are just the people behind the wheel of traditional software engineering. But, in fact, they also work with hardware engineering and other specialists to create IoT solutions. Their job is about putting the right team together to solve problems that might not be knowable until it's too late to fix them. They need creativity and foresight, so their company doesn't miss out on an opportunity or bear the brunt of a hefty cost due to inadequate planning.

The IoT is booming today. Millions of products already use it, and there are thousands of software companies which are working on IoT technology for making the lives easier for people by delivering better products and services.

The IoT has a bright future; it is predicted that by 2025, over 30 billion devices will be connected to the Internet, according to experts. It's no wonder that IoT product managers are among the most sought-after professionals. Their roles are to make sure the various pieces of information that are collected by IoT devices are stored, managed, and retrieved in an efficient way. They use their expertise in IT to make sure the products connect with each other properly and perform as expected.

Creating IoT solutions is more demanding than most people imagine. It takes creativity, innovation, and lateral thinking to come up with solutions for complex problems. This is where IoT product managers make a difference. They have to come up with creative solutions to complex problems and tell their engineering colleagues how to build these solutions. It's not an easy job, but someone has to do it!

IoT Product Managers Are the Bridges Between Technologies and Consumers

A lot of people think that IoT product managers work as traditional product managers, who just handle the software side of things instead of the hardware. But, in reality, that's not the case. An IoT product manager has to work with hardware engineers, system engineers, and other specialists to create a product that is user-friendly and easy to use.

IoT technology is relatively new. It is such a broad term that it covers many products and services which are quite different from each other. The only thing they have in common is that they all use Internet connectivity.

How to Propose Creative Solutions to Complex Problems

It's quite difficult to predict what a product will do when it has Internet connectivity. You have to make sure that it offers the right level of security, data storage, and overall performance. All these things have to work in harmony with the rest of the product and the technology behind it. To do this well, you need a good knowledge of IT fundamentals and how the IoT works.

It's also important for an IoT product manager to be able to understand how consumers use products. They find it difficult to use products that are not well designed or not intuitive. We have to make sure our IoT service is easy to use, whether it is using a smartwatch or a smartphone.

The Good, the Bad, and the Awful of IoT Product Management Roles

Product management has come a long way in the past decade. People are becoming more aware of the increased efficiency of such roles. Along with better technology, people want products that are more personalized and easy to use. And this involves the IoT.

According to the Bureau of Labor Statistics, the number of IoT product managers is expected to grow by 19% between 2014 and 2024. That shows how big a role these professionals will play in our lives.

While it might be a good thing that more people are becoming aware of the value of IoT product managers, they haven't quite learned how to do their job yet. There are many different roles that make up the IoT product management profile. People who manage products and services using IoT technology have to be able to do a lot of things that aren't as straightforward as they used to be a few years ago.

Did you know: The Bluetooth standard was created to allow more devices to be connected using a single laptop.

Security is one of the toughest aspects. As a result, the security part of IoT product managers' jobs increased in 2014.

How to Propose Creative Solutions to Complex Problems?

1. **Make your breakthrough innovation**: In order to create incredible and innovative products and services, IoT product managers have to have a good understanding of the needs of consumers. They need to understand how people use technology. What makes a product great is that it solves a problem or an issue in people's lives. They might not be aware of it when they start using the product, but they will figure it out later on. IoT service providers are also responsible for evolving their business models as technology changes over time and market conditions change.

2. **Keep your team engaged**: You have to make sure that your team is engaged and ready to work on your product at the same time. If you want to create the best possible product, you need to get the right people involved. If you have a small team, it makes

sense to find a way to keep everybody working together. With proper planning and communication, it's possible for a small team of IoT product managers, engineers, and designers to create an excellent product in a timely manner.

3. **Make it corrective when you make mistakes**: The most important thing that any product manager needs to do is make sure they learn from their mistakes. A product manager has to be able to think of ways to improve the design of a product or service. This is where you need to make sure that your team is constantly analyzing how people use things and making them better in some way. It's not enough for a product manager just so that they can collect data about how people use the product. They need to make sure they have an idea of how they can make it better.

4. **Create a good understanding of concepts ahead of time**: It's easy to understand new concepts when you are the one doing the research, but it's a bit harder when you are making the product. IoT product managers need to be able to learn about various concepts and technologies in advance so that they can create a good understanding of them before they get started. Many of the new concepts and technologies are quite complex, and they make it even harder to create a good product.

Then you can propose creative solutions to complex problems.

5.6 Four Steps to Launch and Operate a Secure IoT Product

The Internet of Things (IoT) is booming, as it becomes more and more common for everyday consumers to buy things with the main purpose of connecting to the Internet.

Hardware products that utilize IoT technology are one thing that could help grow this trend. One such product is a smart lock that can be easily operated via an app on your phone. As soon as you walk in front of the sensor, it will unlock and the door will open. This product is a real eye-catcher, and you may want to start selling these smart locks. Yet the process of launching and operating a new product can be challenging, so it's best to avoid the most common pitfalls.

In the following, you'll find four tips for how to launch and run IoT smart locks successfully:

1. **Make sure it works**: First of all, your product needs to work properly. It should be easy to set up, install, and use. The product should be implemented in a way that makes it easy to use. For example, how will the customer set his or her password? Is there a physical key that must be kept in order for the door to unlock? A lock without having to keep track of keys can be a great idea, and it's worth testing.

2. **Consider an IoT gateway**: If you're already developing an IoT product, you may want to consider creating an IoT gateway – a device that allows your smart lock to connect with the network. The IoT gateway makes it easier to watch over your product and monitor the status of all devices.

143

3. **Ensure security is built in**: Security is a huge concern when it comes to connecting your product to the Internet. The same applies for smart locks – you don't want strangers to be able to unlock and enter your home just because they downloaded an app! Therefore, always keep in mind that IoT security must be built in from the very start – this will save you lots of time trying to upgrade or patch existing products later on.

4. **Consider licensing deals**: If you want to be able to sell your smart lock to local stores, you'll need a patent license and distribution rights. Getting the patents, license, and distribution rights can be challenging, so it's worth asking around if someone already has the rights for your product. It may be worth looking for a licensing deal with other companies that have already obtained the necessary patents. This will make it easier for you to launch and operate your IoT smart lock in future.

The preceding four tips will help you avoid the most common mistakes that cause IoT products to face problems after launch. If you follow them carefully, your smart lock will be a huge success.

CHAPTER 6

IoT Product Marketing

When your company or your team wants to do the IoT product marketing, you need to know that it can bring many challenges – some of which are a challenge for you and your team even before you start the marketing process. You need to plan everything from the beginning so it won't be a big headache later on. Here are some tips on how to do IoT product marketing the right way!

1. **Understand your unique value propositions**: Understanding what is the specific value proposition of your product will help you to analyze exactly what and whom you are going to market in. It is important to understand which customer segments you are going to target. For example, you can target those customers who are expecting a very low latency or superfast speed data delivery or those who really need reliability, etc. It is also important when you're looking for the right market channels. There have been some issues with channel selection at different stages of development.

2. **Your competition can save or destroy your business**: You need to identify your competitors for the IoT product market. The thing about being in a new IoT product marketing environment is that your competition could be new and growing fast. This is where you can grow your business, but you need to be wary of your competition.

© Padmaraj Nidagundi 2022
P. Nidagundi, *The IoT Product Manager*, https://doi.org/10.1007/978-1-4842-8631-9_6

3. **Learn to monitor your competitors**: At this point, you should have a good idea about the market channel and who your competitors for the IoT product marketing are. You will then be able to monitor these competitors. Monitor their strengths, weaknesses, and, most importantly, how they are doing it. Think of how your customer is going to find you and the right value proposition. Then look at the way your competition do their IoT product marketing. This is a great way to get inspiration since they are at exactly what you want to achieve!

4. **What are the features and benefits of your product?** Most IoT product marketing companies put emphasis on the features or benefits that their products offer. But this is not enough because many people do not consider these as valuable and sometimes they are not even aware of them. You can develop a long list of features or benefits that your product has. But you also need to focus on the strengths and weaknesses that your product has.

5. **Scaling up faster than competitors**: Big companies have much more resources and capability compared to anyone else. This is why they are able to scale up faster and get bigger ideas in the market. However, they might not be as good at providing excellent value as smaller players. So, it is important that you focus on scaling up your business as fast as possible by offering great value to the customer.

6. **Market research and product development**:
   Usually IoT product marketing companies use a
   combination of qualitative and quantitative market
   research. More often than not, companies that
   have the best market research are able to get good
   information about the market, the customer's needs,
   and the products. This is because they have made
   sure to ask the right questions at the right time.

IOT PRODUCT MARKETING

7. **IoT online customer support 24/7**: You might think
   that you will be able to get immediate help if you
   have an urgent need for it. But for some reason, this
   is not always the case. Having a way to request help
   or support from your marketing team will look great
   in the end when you are trying to achieve the best
   results possible.

8. **Follow up with your customers**: You can't just send
   an email and expect it to do its job. Create a follow-
   up process in order to have a way of maintaining the

contact with your customers. Sending out emails can be good, but you also need to make sure that you are available on more channels.

9. **Make it easy for everyone to come back to you**: If someone takes the time to find and contact your company, they want their problem solved as soon as possible. If you are able to do this, then most likely they will go back to you when they require your product or service again.

10. **Use data in your advantage**: When you are trying to figure out the effectiveness of your marketing, you need to start by measuring it. To make doing this easier, you will have to install a good IoT product marketing platform. This can allow you to track conversion rate and make better decisions. In short, this will help you achieve more sales results.

11. **Be flexible when it comes to the products**: The product that your company is selling might not always be the same in terms of their quality or design. Your customers might have different needs and expectations. So, they are going to expect the same from your product, but it is important that you can adjust according to what your customers want.

12. **Be better and improve your product constantly**: A lot of companies just stop with the product they have, but this might not be helpful. You need to always be improving your IoT product marketing to make sure that you are getting better results. This will help you to make a great impression on customers and make them understand that your company is going to improve the products they are selling.

13. **Use a good analytics platform**: Analytics can help you in many ways, but it's especially helpful when it comes down to product marketing. This is because you'll be able to see what products are being sold and who your customers are. It is important that you have analytics that can show how much time will the customer take to use your product.

14. **Improve and increase your capacity**: When you need to grow, it is important to improve your capacity and make sure that your company is growing faster than everyone else. Do not just stop at the size and completion of your business; you also need to keep track of how each individual part of the business works.

15. **Tell IoT success stories**: If you want to be known, then you need to tell everyone that your company is doing great. This is why you must have a way to share success stories whenever you can. Customers and potential clients are going to be more interested in doing business with companies who are successful.

16. **Use a good IoT product marketing template**: You need to make sure that everything is organized when it comes down to marketing your business online. You can use quality templates that can help in the creation of your emails and website content. Using a template is a good idea, especially if you are new to the business.

17. **Maintain constant communication with your customers**: You'll be able to feel this if your company isn't doing its job properly. You should make sure that you are answering all of the customer's questions and concerns immediately when they surface. People aren't going to like bringing up issues without having an organization that is ready to deal with these problems.

6.1 What Makes a Good IoT Product

In the present, the Internet of Things industry is booming with countless new technologies that can be used in various ways. The question is, what exactly makes a good IoT product? Or it may be better to ask what are the key factors that should always be considered when launching a new IoT device or service. Here are some general thoughts on making a quality product.

A good IoT product has to have an intuitive user experience. It should be easy to use, even for users not familiar with technology. This is especially important for a mass-market audience, who aren't familiar with this type of product.

A quality IoT device has to be easy to install and maintain. We are talking here about devices that should be used by everyone, both technically experienced and inexperienced users alike.

A quality IoT product has to be secure and compatible with different platforms. This way, it can be integrated in various environments and interact with other devices. A quality IoT product has to have a good design and user interface. It should look good, work great, and be reliable.

An easy way to achieve all of these goals is by using the right tools and technologies. There are plenty of them to choose from, such as microcontrollers, sensors, cloud platforms (like Amazon Web Services), and many more. There are even open source options that anyone can use to build their own device.

An important thing to remember is that there is no single best option for all devices or products. Every good IoT product will have to solve the problems of its particular target market. That's why the correct tool has to be used for every IoT project, even though it may turn out that this choice was not optimal, because it was a bad fit for what was needed.

6.2 IoT Product Marketing Strategy

You might not know it, but the Internet of Things (IoT) is about to change the way we live. These devices take in data from our homes and schools and share it with us, telling us how much water we're using or what time the kids will be home. The IoT can help people with mental health issues by reminding them to take their medication or can help a busy family stay organized by sending a text at bedtime reminding you to set your alarm clock for tomorrow morning.

My job is to help companies understand the technological changes that will take place and how it will fit into their strategies. Although there are many different IoT devices, most are about the same. We've come a long way from the first personal computer and the rise of smartphones, but here's what we know and don't know about how we will use these products in the future.

What We Know

"The Internet of Things" was coined by Kevin Ashton, who was Intel's director of emerging technology at the time. Today, Ashton is the founder and CEO of the Smarter Cities Institute, a nonprofit organization that aims to make cities safer, healthier, more efficient, and environmentally sustainable.

The IoT is a combination of devices – computers, sensors, lighting systems, and video cameras (among others) – that all communicate with each other using subtle signals. These signals can be as simple as light or motion changes or as complex as adjusting a thermostat 10 degrees in order to save energy. The IoT is already in our homes, businesses, and schools. As more devices are added to our existing systems, the IoT will become a part of every aspect of our lives.

These devices can be connected by wireless signals, or they can be networked by computer with cables or through the cloud. They all share information on usage, location, and activity. This can provide a number of benefits such as saving energy, understanding traffic movement, and making infrastructure more efficient.

For example, connected devices help us conserve energy by knowing when we're using the most power in our home. The system can then adjust to save us more money and make our homes more comfortable.

With connected devices in transportation systems, we can monitor traffic and use dynamic signs to warn drivers about upcoming road problems. This saves time for commuters and helps ease traffic flow, reducing the number of accidents.

What We Don't Know

It's true that the IoT can save us energy, time, and money. But this technology also poses some serious threats that are difficult to predict. Hackers could take control of our devices and use them for their own purposes, causing real problems.

Another danger is having someone intercept information intended for another individual. This could create problems if an employee sends a personal document to her boss by accident or wastes time when someone sends a private message to the wrong person.

All of this may sound like science fiction, but experts agree that the IoT is here to stay. Given what we know now, we need to work out the best way to use it in future products and services.

IoT technology is still developing. We don't yet know all the benefits or consequences of using these devices. As time goes on, we will be able to address these concerns and make our lives easier as more people purchase and use IoT products.

Companies will be challenged to stay at the forefront of IoT development as they create new products that can benefit industries and customers. By staying on top of this technology, businesses will be able to create unique products and services that provide solutions for companies and customers in ways that couldn't be imagined just a few years ago.

What Are the Factors That Will Affect the Success of Your IoT Products?

What are some of the problems that might occur when using these devices? How could they affect your target customers? How can you reduce the risk of that happening?

How do you plan to develop a marketing strategy for IoT products in your company? What steps do you take to implement this strategy? How do you make sure it's successful? Why is it important to focus on these issues now rather than later? What training do you give employees on?

It's very difficult to predict the future. However, you will be able to use what you learn here in your job and in your daily life. By planning ahead, you can make the best of this new technology and ensure that you'll be positioned well for the future.

IOT PRODUCT MARKETING STRATEGY

Where to Sell IoT Products?

IoT products are becoming more and more popular by the day. How should companies be approaching this growing demand? Increasingly, IoT experts say that businesses need to think about how IoT devices can be used in their company's ecosystem. What does that mean for you?

Take, for example, a company that uses GPS devices to keep track of their fleet of trucks. By integrating these devices with their software and other IoT devices, they can create a strategy that will help the company save time, money, and resources.

When you're selling your IoT products, you need to know how they fit in with your customers' existing systems. It's not enough to just know how your products work on their own. You need to understand how they can help your customers run an efficient business.

The IoT has the potential to create new business models. To make this possible, businesses need to understand how the technology can help them sell their products in other industries.

IoT devices have the power to change everything we know about running a business. But it's not simply a case of adapting these devices to fit in with your business. With the right business practices and marketing strategies, you can create an IoT ecosystem that will allow your company to survive for years to come.

6.3 IoT Trends: Revenue and New IoT Business Models

Who Benefits from an IoT Business Model

Developers, manufacturers, and consumers all benefit from an IoT business model. Developers are essential to these business models because they are the ones who create the software and devices that run on the Internet of Things. Consumers benefit because they can use a wide range of connected devices while manufacturers enjoy a boost in revenue as they create new products that utilize Internet of Things technologies.

How to Create an IoT Business Model

There are many ways to create a business model around Internet of Things technologies. The first step is creating a prototype that showcases what you can do with the technology in question. Once you have your prototype, you need to think about how you can improve on your current prototype or make it work better. These are important steps involved in creating an IoT business model because they help you decide which niche or industry segment would best suit your new technology and how it should be marketed.

How an IoT Business Model Can Increase Revenue

Internet of Things technologies are everywhere, and they are making a big splash in the market. A business model based around your particular technology will allow you to capitalize off this popularity and increase your revenue significantly. For example, if you create a car with smart suspension which can be remotely adjusted, this would be a great way to offer your customers an improved experience in their cars.

Generating recurring revenue is a critical part of an IoT business model. This revenue is generated by those connected devices that can be operated remotely, such as thermostats or lighting systems, and the data they generate. This data can be tailored to your consumers because you can use it to tailor your products and services based on their needs.

The key to an IoT business model is creating a unique value proposition for your target audience. By doing this, you will be able to attain mass appeal because you will have something that all consumers want.

Generating new revenue from discovery and monetization
opportunities for an IoT business model is dependent on the previous
steps of creating a prototype and improving on it. After market testing
and refinement, you can have plenty of ideas for ways to monetize your
connected devices. It is important to be aware that you will have competition
in your industry, but the good news is that the market is constantly growing.

Incorporating the Internet of Things into your business is always
going to be a huge benefit, and it can be done in so many ways. The
opportunities that you have with this type of technology are endless and
can only be used properly if you understand them. An IoT business model
should always start out with the idea that there are more opportunities
than there are problems, so it is important to look at these opportunities
from a whole new perspective.

Generating new revenue from data collection and data selling for
an IoT business model is available to those who have created new products
and services. With subscriptions and analytics, you have the ability to know
what your customers are doing and how your products or services work
with them. This is a great way to monetize because you can charge for new
products, upgrades, or services that help your customer's lives improve.

156

There are experts in every field that can provide valuable advice, but thematic analysis of current trends will greatly assist you in creating an IoT business model that works.

Future Trends in the IoT

1) The world is more connected than ever with 7.5 billion people using the Internet. A large majority of these users come from developed countries, but the trend is that developing countries are catching up fast. This change in user behavior will add a huge amount of devices to the Internet and will require IoT infrastructure to be able to stream the data from these devices. This infrastructure may require an overhaul as traditional methods don't work well with so many devices coming online at once.

2) The IoT will also change the way that businesses and consumers interact with technology. Many of these changes are already happening as we speak, for example, in feature phones as iPhones pull them out of people's pockets and TVs become smart assistants to the user. Both of these changes show how consumer behavior will change once connected devices are ubiquitous.

3) The Web has become a more social experience with more people interacting through websites and services on their smartphones instead of opening a web browser. This has changed the way people use the Internet, and if these trends continue, then the future of the IoT will be centered around connected devices that do not require a smartphone.

4) The Internet of Things also has a lot of potential in healthcare. On a global scale, healthcare is still lacking in many areas, but as technology advances, it becomes more accessible to those who need it.

5) Security is an important part of any business model and must be addressed when implementing an IoT business model. This is not only because of hacking but also because of privacy concerns. The ease of use that the IoT brings to customers may cause more people to give away their personal information unknowingly. This can be seen with cloud services, which are growing in popularity each day.

6) The Internet of Things allows devices and appliances to be connected to each other, but this can present another problem; many companies will have a hard time creating their own platform when there are already so many available all connected to the Internet.

7) The IoT brings many benefits to customers and the companies that offer products and services. If consumers are happy, then they will spend more money with these companies as they will receive a better experience, which could translate into immediate boosts in revenue.

8) Device manufacturers often struggle with connectivity issues, and there is no clear guideline for how to fix them. The way that these devices are connected can cause security concerns and cause the customer to have a bad experience with their item.

"The Internet of Things" is a paradigm shift in the way we will live and interact with each other and the world around us. This paradigm shift is being fueled by an increase in three fundamental areas: exponential improvement in technology, an explosion in data, and the ability for anyone to connect these devices virtually anywhere. Combined, this is creating a world where everything from cars to coffee makers is connected to the Internet – allowing us access to these devices from anywhere and at any time.

How to Create New IoT Business Models

Step 1: Create an IoT prototype

The most important step in creating an IoT business model is to make a product that actually works. This will allow you to identify the right idea for your product and to test it out with actual users. When you start building, don't just think about the connected device itself, but create a full ecosystem around it. This will allow you to test your business model before it goes into production. It will also help you to see if there is demand for the product, which can be very helpful.

Step 2: Take your business model offline

When you have a working prototype and are testing the market, it's time to take your business model offline. This will involve taking your prototype outside of the Web and into real life. This means going to a conference or trade show and setting up a booth in front of potential customers. It is also important to talk to people in person rather than send out cold emails. Having a presence can get you a lot of secondhand sales because real people will come up to your booth and tell you about it.

Step 3: Create some buzz about your product

If your prototype seems like it will be successful, then start looking for places that would be helpful in promoting the product. This can be as simple as sending an email out to a news outlet or getting on Reddit and submitting content about your product. But don't let the buzz go to your head. It's important to keep testing your business model and finding ways to improve it.

Step 4: Put together a marketing plan

Even if you have come up with a product that you think will be successful, you have to market it in order for it to become real. This means creating a marketing plan that will help to promote your product and getting people excited about it. This will allow you to determine the target audience and the best way to promote your product. It can also help you to create sales, which is especially important when creating a new business model.

Step 5: Get help from an expert

Once you begin marketing your product, it can be tough finding a way to get your sales numbers up. This is where it pays off to hire a specialist who has been in this business before. They will be able to teach you what you need to know in order to get your marketing done in the right way.

Step 6: Create a business model

The hardest part of creating an IoT business model is figuring out how to profit from it. Once you have found a way to promote your product, it's time to figure out how you can make money on it. This usually involves creating a subscription model where the customer pays a monthly fee in exchange for access to your service.

Step 7: Create a website and start selling

Once you have created a marketing plan, it's time to create a website. This will allow you to market your product and to make sure that everyone who is interested in it can find out more information about it. You can also put together a sales page which will include pictures of the product, how it works, and how much it costs. It's also best to use different types of media on your site in order to encourage visitors to go through the purchase process.

CHAPTER 7

Government Regulation on IoT

The Internet of Things is a world-changing phenomenon that is sweeping the globe. As the number of connected devices increases, so does the complexity and potential for malfunctions – and, consequently, regulation. Governments are scrambling to come up with laws and regulations to keep up with IoT's breakneck pace. However, the most significant and major challenge is that the definitions of "things" and "connectivity" are constantly evolving.

Upon further reflection, it becomes quite apparent why government regulations on the IoT are so difficult to carry out. In some governments defined that IoT as "any device with an embedded computer" or "any device connected to the Internet." Other governments defined that IoT by actual physical devices, such as a refrigerator, instead of a software-based device. This creates a problem when it comes to identifying the physical devices that need to be regulated.

7.1 European Union (EU) Laws for IoT

In September of 2017, the European Union (EU) issued a report on IoT after working with its Scientific Committee and Council of Europe's Steering Committee. This report provides clarification on what an Internet

© Padmaraj Nidagundi 2022
P. Nidagundi, *The IoT Product Manager*, https://doi.org/10.1007/978-1-4842-8631-9_7

of Things is and how it should be defined in hopes to create standards regarding manufacturer liability, security, interoperability, and sustainable development.

The EU report recommends that the scope of IoT should encompass devices with a physical interface, and they should be classified by their functions and operations. This is quite broad, and many IoT devices already exist that do not fall under this category. For example, a wearable headset could be considered an IoT device if it has an embedded computer, even though the device doesn't necessarily have a physical interface (i.e., it is worn on a person's head like earphones).

In addition, the scope of IoT should include any type of network-connected device that can be remotely configured, reprogrammed, and controlled. The report also recommends that functionalities be included in the classification framework. A network-connected device can have many different functionalities, such as environmental sensing or targeted advertising.

The EU report does not define IoT by specific types of devices but rather by particular purpose/functionality and connectivity technologies based on a classification framework. This classification framework can be used to classify any type of IoT device, which is a significant improvement over the current approach.

The EU report also briefly discusses security, interoperability, and sustainability issues. The European Commission (EC) will issue further recommendations on these issues. As IoT grows and becomes more critical, security must be a top priority for government regulation to ensure safety and reliability of the industry. One way the EU can improve IoT cybersecurity is by adopting common industry standards for security and interoperability of devices.

The boundary of IoT is the physical length or the distance that a device can communicate with another device. The boundary length is determined by the type of devices being used to determine the distance. The standard kilometers (m) used in measuring distance are based on

International Telecommunication Union's (ITU) recommendations. In addition, there are many other mapping and routing protocols used in IoT devices out there, which also dictate the size of boundaries.

7.2 United States (US) Laws for IoT

In the United States, the Federal Communications Commission (FCC) has been working to define the IoT. The FCC believes that the IoT is a network-connected device with a unique ID and the ability to communicate with other information and communication devices. In February of 2018, the FCC formed an Internet of Things (IoT) Task Force to resolve issues around interoperability, privacy, and technical standardization.

GOVERNMENT REGULATION

The FCC identifies five main focus areas for IoT:

A. **Protecting and promoting interoperability**: The United States has a rich history of private sector innovation coupled with critical government leadership, creating an environment where industry can achieve rapid growth and technical advancement. The IoT is an area where industry continues to innovate, but current limitations in interoperability of products and services present challenges in the market. The FCC recognizes the need to foster an environment that provides the benefits of interoperability and flexibility while ensuring consumer protection and appropriate levels of service. The FCC has two key goals in this area: first, to ensure that consumers are presented with a variety of services and choices on how they access digital connectivity; second, to promote a high degree of digital privacy/security.

B. **Promoting innovation**: The FCC recognizes the important role IoT can play in stimulating innovation and promoting new ways for consumers to enjoy broadband connectivity. The FCC will encourage the construction of innovative and relevant standards which promote interoperability, safety, and security. The FCC also seeks to ensure that consumers are presented with a variety of services and choices from a diverse range of wireless/wireline service providers.

C. **Protecting consumers**: Consumers are best served when the marketplace for IoT is free from unscrupulous actors or other deceptive tactics that may lead consumers to believe they have purchased a particular device or service when they do not. The FCC will continue to work with consumer groups and industry members to ensure that consumers are not misled by deceptive or unfair practices related to the marketing and sale of devices for IoT.

D. **Promoting resilience**: The Internet has fostered innovation in many industries, but its architecture can be a source of vulnerabilities if not well protected. The Commission will help build resilience into networks by encouraging connectivity using various forms of the IoT and smart home services. The Commission will also promote adoption of IoT and smart home devices by assisting in the development of standards for sensors and devices.

E. **Promoting cybersecurity**: The IoT provides new opportunities for the government and industry to share information, reduce vulnerabilities, and improve overall cyber hygiene. The Commission will utilize its existing cybersecurity resources to support these goals. As part of this effort, the FCC will coordinate with federal agencies and other stakeholders to develop a framework for protecting connected devices from cybersecurity threats.

The FCC will also continue to support other agencies that are working on IoT-related issues. For example, the Department of Homeland Security (DHS) runs a Cybersecurity and Intelligence Integration Center that focuses on IoT-related security issues. Also, the Federal Trade Commission (FTC) has developed a Cybersecurity Framework for Consumer Technology Manufacturers and Third Party Service Providers.

7.3 Canada Laws for IoT

In Canada, there is no legislation defining or regulating the Internet of Things. The Government of Canada works individually with each industry to ensure the security of devices.

Canada IoT Sector Market Size and Forecast (2013–2023)

The Canadian Internet of Things market, comprising everything from smart washing machines to connected cars, is expected to grow from $6 billion in 2014 to $22 billion by 2025. It will be valued at $153 billion by the end of 2024, growing at a CAGR of 10.7%. The growth of the market will be driven by high-end applications such as smart thermostats, connected fitness equipment, and other smart home appliances, connected security systems, and automated parking. The global nature of the Canadian industry will also underpin its growth with over 50% of all IoT devices produced outside Canada.

Canada Laws for IoT

1. The Government of Canada will make available $100 million to support research and development (R&D) projects in the areas of cybersecurity and privacy/digital rights management.

2. The government will also create an IoT Project Accelerator to develop partnerships between industry and academia as well as conduct outreach activities with stakeholders.

3. The government will also create a new IoT Challenge Prizes Program over the next five years to support world-class, innovative, and disruptive ideas for the development of connected devices, platforms, and services that contribute to a more dynamic and resilient economy.

4. The federal government will cooperate with provinces and territories on supporting the growth of IoT-related industries including:

5. The government will also work with private sector partners to apply IoT solutions to support innovation, productivity, competitiveness, and business growth across a range of industries.

6. The government will continue to engage in international fora such as the Internet of Things (IoT) Standards Working Group that is cochaired by Canada and the United States.

7. The government will support the development of IoT solutions in sectors such as healthcare, education, energy, and transportation.

7.4 Incorporate Standards and Regulations in Your IoT Product Strategy

IoT devices are likely to be part of our everyday lives in the near future, and there is a lot of work to do around their adoption, security, and privacy. There's also a lot of work ahead for product makers. The industry needs to focus on where it can truly find value and how it can be an enabler for people, not just another technology that collects data about us.

A lot of investment and excitement is surrounding the IoT. It's an exciting time for entrepreneurs, makers, developers, and technologists all over the world. With such a revolutionary technology that will undoubtedly impact our lives, we must start thinking about how to ensure standards are being applied properly and what kind of regulations we'll need to ensure user privacy and security.

The first step is getting everyone on the same page – developers, entrepreneurs, and business folks are starting to figure out privacy concerns, security risks, and government regulations in specific industries. The good news is that the situation is improving; more and more people are starting to realize that we need to do something about it.

We can take a lot of inspiration from what happened with the telecom industry in the 1980s and 1990s. Back then, I was working for a couple of government agencies, helping them navigate through some of the regulations that impacted their industries. It was a big job to manage the quality control and be ready for when AT&T, MCI, Sprint, and others started rolling out IP-only services to their users in the early 1990s.

The first thing we had to figure out was where it all was going. How would we make sure that the technologies we were providing service to our citizens with were compliant with regulations?

After some thought, there ended up being five different standards bodies. The first was the Federal Communications Commission (FCC), which mandated the switching protocols – between cities, states, countries, and carriers. The second was the National Institute of Standards and Technology (NIST), which focused on security and privacy. The third organization was called the Open Systems Interconnection (OSI) model, which dictated how everything would work internally in IT.

The fourth standard was from the International Organization for Standardization (ISO) that outlined how everything communicated between IT systems. And the fifth standard was the Open Source model, which was based on a lot of open source technology.

Looking back, it seems pretty simple to build standards into technology; but back then, no one had done anything like that before. It came with a major learning curve for all of us. Governments, businesses, and citizens had to learn how new technologies can impact their lives and how they should deal with privacy and security.

This was a huge challenge, but it set the tone of how to properly address concerns around standards compliance and regulation. A few years later, I found myself having similar conversations with companies in the mobile network industry. These discussions were on how to move from 2G technology to 3G, 4G and bring in 5G technologies.

These conversations were not as difficult because it was obvious that we had to change something. There were a lot of issues surrounding the transition from 2G to 3G technologies; the industry needed to ensure that end users had better quality phones and faster data speeds.

There was a ton of work that went into standardizing and making sure things played together. We did not have to deal with a lot of security or privacy concerns as there have been far fewer issues around mobile networks than around other technologies (not any less, though).

There was a similar learning curve for us in the mobile network industry and leading up to the introduction of 4G LTE. In mobile networks, it was not difficult to figure out how devices were going to communicate with each other – things like how the phone would talk to the tower, who would pay for that connection, and how data speeds were going to be delivered.

We had a lot of trials and errors until it was all figured out. There were a lot of regulations, rules, and laws to take into effect. To make sure things aligned with regulations, the US government passed the Telecommunications Act of 1996.

In that Act, there were a number of interesting stipulations: "...to foster competition," "commercialization," "universal service," and "interconnection." These were very similar to what we hear today about the need for standards. We still see a lot of these same initiatives being pushed for standards compliance and adoption.

These concepts can get lost in the implementation of technology and the process of actually getting things done. There is no doubt that technology can be very disruptive in many industries, but we've got to ensure the technology is meeting user needs properly, is secure, meets privacy regulations, and aligns with other industry efforts such as privacy laws and regulations.

This is where the next stage in standards compliance will come from. One of the things you will see more of over the coming years is government regulations to ensure user privacy and security. There are regulations for data privacy, security, and compliance with industry standards that are already in place; there are quite a few others on their way.

It's going to be an exciting time. I'm excited to watch how these new technologies grow and see how they will impact our lives as people, businesses, and citizens.

7.5 IoT Product and Data Security

Information technologies are transforming and improving our daily lives. Within a few years, the Internet of Things (IoT) will be integrated into everything we do – and it comes with its own vulnerabilities. With the number of connected devices on the rise, hackers have started targeting IoT product vendors to gain access to the data collected by these devices. In this chapter, we provide insight into IoT product and data security trends. We also present three recommended strategies for staying one step ahead of your competitors and remaining in control of your personal information resources.

Need of IoT Data Security

The Internet of Things (IoT) is transforming and improving our daily lives by connecting devices that were previously separate or not networked to the Internet in any way. We now have devices to track and monitor things like our fitness activity, energy usage, home security, and even pets. Yet with this range of data comes a new set of security challenges for device vendors and consumers alike.

The security vulnerabilities of IoT devices have been building up over the years. In 2015, a study by CSO revealed that 50% of IoT devices come with a default set of credentials, and in most cases, the credentials are not changed. That means it's very easy for an unauthorized person to access the device and extract personal information like usernames, passwords, and credit card details. By nature, IoT devices are also fragile, which makes them vulnerable to malicious attacks.

An unauthorized person can access an IoT device using a number of entry points, including Wi-Fi and Bluetooth connections. Hackers can use a low-cost off-the-shelf device to send malicious software that allows them to access sensitive data. For example, they could then extract the user's personal information at will.

Trends and Key Concerns Related to Data Security in IoT

According to a study from McAfee, more than half of enterprises are planning to launch a digital strategy this year in order to "go digital" and reinvent their business. But the Internet of Things (IoT) could become the biggest security threat they have ever seen.

The IoT is already here. It's used for registering our cars and managing home appliances but also for monitoring our fitness activity or placing our home under surveillance. In the future, it will encompass a large number of other things – things that are connected to the Internet and that can communicate with one another. Despite the fact that many IoT devices already exist, there is still a long way to go before we reach an IoT-ready world.

With the IoT's massive potential, more and more vendors are focusing on making their products secure by creating stronger security profiles. So far, however, the focus has been primarily on IT security issues. For example, they might have implemented an IoT policy to protect their data center.

In the future, companies will need to strengthen the security profiles of their IoT devices, too. One example is a smart kettle that can turn on your home appliances when you are running out of water. If someone could get access to this device, they'll be able to turn it on and use the power outlet for other purposes. That's why, in the future, all IoT products will need strong security profiles.

However, we also want to provide you with strategies to improve the security of your IoT devices and keep your data safe on the Internet. In our opinion, three key strategies are worth discussing:

1. **Do not trust the device manufacturer**: Authorized users should only connect their device to the network after they have verified that there are no unauthorized connections. This is best done by the device manufacturer. However, there is another approach that makes a lot of sense: do not trust the device manufacturer at all.

   The problem with this strategy is that IoT vendors have to take on the responsibility of protecting their customers' data. After all, they are in charge of keeping unauthorized connections away from their customers and devices. So, they need to implement solutions that make it impossible for unauthorized devices and people to connect to the network in any way.

2. **Monitor critical connections**: To prevent unauthorized connections to their computers, a smartphone user should make use of VPNs and other applications. However, IoT devices have fewer opportunities for protected access: they do not have the services that allow us to hide our location or restrict access to the Internet.

The idea is to monitor critical connections (such as Wi-Fi, Bluetooth, and Ethernet). For example, in order to detect any unauthorized connection attempts from other devices, a smart light bulb needs to monitor whether it is connected to the network or not. If an unauthorized device tries to connect to the network, the light bulb needs to realize this and take action accordingly. If it's a malware code that was sent over the Internet, it can be deleted.

3. **Use a distributed system**: Data security on the Internet has always been a big challenge for public cloud providers who operate data centers connected to the Internet. They have to spend a lot of money on IT security tools, because one missed opportunity would make them vulnerable to attackers.

In the future, however, most of the tasks that need to be done in order to keep IoT devices secure can be accomplished by third parties without any danger to the IoT device itself. To work together with us and contribute to keeping your data safe on the Internet, please visit DeviceSecurityProject.com for more information about the three strategies mentioned earlier.

As IoT devices become more popular, security vulnerabilities are growing as well. The IoT is an ecosystem where your own smart devices connect to other smart devices and store, share, and analyze data collected from those devices. As a result, hackers can gain access to that data. In order to prevent these attacks, it is not enough to only connect the devices to the network in a secure way. It is also necessary to focus on what you have stored on those devices and try to protect that data as much as possible.

7.6 IoT Product Manager Skills for Future

There are a lot of skills that are necessary for success in the IoT. Here is a list of some of the most important skills you need to learn and provide to organizations looking for an IoT product manager! With these skills, you'll be able to stand out as an expert in this field.

1. **Understanding the IoT for beginners**: The Internet of Things market has become more sophisticated and is growing at a rapid pace. There are more products and offerings being introduced on a daily basis in this industry! It is important to understand what it takes to make a comprehensive IoT product that can be used by all.

2. **Startup approach**: You also have to understand the difference between products that are viable and those that are not successful. The first step to becoming an IoT startup product manager is to understand how to get your product introduced. This doesn't just include the product but also the entire ecosystem!

3. **Product management and DevOps skills**: You will have to have a strong grasp of both product management and development at all levels! You need to be able to juggle between both fields and understand their differences. You should be able to explain why each of them is important and how you will use them together in a way that is beneficial to the organization building your IoT product!

4. **Product ownership**: You will have to have the ability to lead, organize, and manage a product's team.

5. **AI and ML skills**: The ability to understand artificial intelligence and machine learning concepts is extremely important for IoT product management! You need to be able to teach your team about these skills so that they are aware of what you are doing and why.

6. **Data visualization – A critical skill**: You need to be able to understand how the data you are collecting from various sources will be used. You need a visual representation of the data and how they will be analyzed so that they can be presented effectively!

7. **Innovation/ideation/design for UI/UX**: You need to be able to develop ideas, sketch prototypes, and do usability testing in order to create products that are easy to use and will be adopted by a variety of users.

8. **Understanding of product life cycle management (PLM)**: You will have to understand how each stage of the product life cycle works while working with a team. This includes R&D, manufacturing, support, and adaptations needed over time!

9. **Understanding markets around the world**: In order to be an IoT product manager, you need to be a master at understanding how other markets work. You will not just have to focus on your own domestic market but also on foreign markets that you could use as potential customers!

10. **Automation/provisioning/development**: You will also need to understand how automation works, why it is important for your product, and how you can be a part of the ecosystem that will make this happen.

11. **Customer service – Another must-have skill**: You need to know how to deliver excellent customer service. Doing so is crucial in keeping the brand and company's customers happy! You need to constantly be improving customer support even if it takes you time away from other responsibilities.

7.7 IoT Products in 2030

This chapter shows you what the Internet of Things will look like in 2030 and which companies will still be around!

In 2030, people will have had some sort of "IoT device" on their personal or in their living space for more than half a decade. They become more affordable and accessible each year, as components shrink and new innovative ideas are explored. User-friendly apps, devices, and services make these products significantly easier for you to use.

The following products will be around in 2030, which technology companies that are still around till 30 years later:

- eBook reader – Amazon Kindle (Amazon)

- Phone – Apple iPhone (Apple)

- Websites/Tumblr chapters – Tumblr (Tumblr)

- e-ticketing system – Concourse Saver (Concourse Saver)

- Internet service providers (ISPs)/web hosting and servers – Cloudflare Communications Ltd. (Cloudflare)

- Internet radio – TuneIn (TuneIn)

- Bluetooth devices – Sony Xperia Sola (Sony)

- Smart speakers – Smart speakers from Amazon and Google (Amazon, Google)

- Jeep/SUV – Jeep Wrangler/Grand Cherokee (J.D. Power and Associates)

- Mobile games – Mobile games from Apple, Google, and Samsung Electronics mobile division (Apple, Google, Samsung)

- Luggage – Samsung Suitcase (Samsung)

- Watches – Smartwatches from Apple, Google, and Samsung Electronics mobile division (Apple, Google, Samsung)

- Portable battery charger – Energizer Powermat (Energizer)

- Home security system – Brilliant Fence Home Security System (Brilliant Fence)

- Digital camera/camera phone – Digital camera from a small company like GoPro (GoPro)

In the year 2030, people will still be taking pictures with their smartphone cameras. Companies from around the world will be trying to dominate the market by providing more and better cameras with more and better features – the main one being waterproofing, which will make it harder for companies to compete against each other.

Our smartphone camera has changed our culture in the past five years of its existence, from "No Selfie" culture to "The Perfect Selfie."

The camera is a very important piece of equipment used for photography because it can bring to life what we have in our brain.

What will the next camera be like in the year 2030? We may never know. That is how much change and innovation occurs in the year 2030.

The biggest trend for cameras this year will be the rise of 360-degree cameras. This is a camera that can rotate and take a picture from any angle. This will be very useful if you are traveling and need to take pictures without getting out of your vehicle in an awkward position.

People will still be using their smartphones to take pictures, because they produce excellent images with great lighting. The brands will be fighting over the best camera phone.

Google is a competitor to Apple and Samsung, because they are very innovative in terms of their digital products and services. Even though they are not known as a big camera company, they are making a name for themselves in the digital world.

Around 2030, IoT products will bring new business opportunity and create industrial revolution. For example, when the mobile Internet and smartphone started to emerge, social networking sites emerged as the next big thing. The same thing will happen this time.

Innovative ideas and ingenious business models will keep emerging and create disruptive effects on a global scale. This is what we are seeing at this moment.

The majority of IoT product vendors need to increase their marketing investment in order to promote their product aggressively to the potential consumers. Marketing plays a vital role in the success of any company's products.

Follow Along the Journey

This is a perfect book for every product manager who wants to enhance their skills as an Internet of Things product manager. I am sure that this book will grab your attention straight away and make you think about the basic things associated with the Internet of Things, its products, and how professionals should lead their lives as well as customers.

This book is going to help you a lot in your life as an IoT product manager. You will be able to take this book with yourself anywhere you go, and I am sure that you are going to enjoy reading it. With this, the author has also provided a self-interview section, and these are perfect for every IoT product manager.

I hope that you will enjoy reading this book as much as the author did while writing it.

I would recommend this book even if you are not currently working in the industry but rather just thinking of changing your career.

Before I finish reading this book! Let us make some notes to follow up:

Why do I need to become an IoT product manager?

© Padmaraj Nidagundi 2022
P. Nidagundi, *The IoT Product Manager*, https://doi.org/10.1007/978-1-4842-8631-9

How to become an IoT product manager in a tech company?

_____

_____

_____

How to do IoT product manager work in the agile era?

_____

_____

_____

_____

Why I need to know about leadership and communication

_____

_____

_____

_____

What are the main IoT product manager skills?

_____

_____

_____

_____

_____

How do IoT product managers do leadership and communication?

_____

_____

_____

_____

_____

_____

How to fix IoT over engineering problems?

_____

_____

_____

_____

_____

_____

_____

How does an IoT product manager work on managing a product backlog?

_____

_____

_____

_____

_____

_____

Difference between IoT development vs. software development

How does an IoT product manager take the product strategic decisions?

How an IoT product manager makes simple proposal, creative solutions to complex problems

How an IoT product manager makes critical decisions

What are my three main mistakes in the last three months?

My top 11 takeaways from this book

FOLLOW ALONG THE JOURNEY

_____

_____

_____

_____

_____

_____

_____

-

Suggestion for Future Work

One of the most discussed topics and buzzwords in recent years is "the Internet of Things." The IoT, also known as by a number of other monikers, refers to an interconnected web of physical devices that share information and data. This can be referred to as an Internet-connected device's connectivity with other devices or technologies without requiring human interaction.

The future should hold many opportunities for the IoT to develop and grow in our society. However, there are also a few different scenarios that could happen. This book looks at the various opportunities and threats for the IoT, how it will change our present and future, and how we can benefit from it.

Starting out with the threats, what can create a threat to seemingly beneficial Internet of Things? The main concern over using this technology is privacy. As with any other device that collects information, it can be possible to gather information on people without their consent. Although some devices are being designed to keep private data safe, there is still much to be done in order to overcome this issue.

Although security concerns are a major concern, there are many benefits to the IoT as well. This technology has the potential to improve our lives. It could allow us to take better care of our health and prevent disease. It can even reduce crime and make the lives of law enforcement officials easier by increasing their ability to connect with any information they need while they're on duty.

The Internet of Things is also predicted to help with tasks such as energy management and scheduling. Having the ability to control your appliances or systems from a single device will be beneficial for both

© Padmaraj Nidagundi 2022
P. Nidagundi, *The IoT Product Manager*, https://doi.org/10.1007/978-1-4842-8631-9

energy companies and people. You'll be able to control your thermostat from your office at work or even on a business trip, for example.

One of the most important benefits that the Internet of Things can have is that it can improve efficiency in various industries, especially the manufacturing industry. There are many examples of how the IoT can be beneficial for these industries. For example, a sensor that monitors radiation and produces heat when it receives a harmful level of radiation from MRI machines can be used to stop those machines from producing too much heat and thus wasting energy. This idea is one example of how we will see the IoT play a major role in our manufacturing industries.

The Internet of Things is anticipated to contribute to more than just the manufacturing industry, however. It could also play a significant role in many other areas of society. One example of how the Internet of Things can be beneficial in our lives is with the military. There may be robots and drones that assist our military troops in the future. Drawing an example, there's a new robotic firefighting truck that can deliver water to those fighting fires. It can also fill up a tank before it heads out on a mission, so its crew doesn't have to go back to headquarters for more water.

The Internet of Things could also lead to advancements in transportation such as autonomous vehicles. This technology is also predicted to help reduce traffic jams, as there may be cars that can communicate with one another and share information. This will allow them to avoid traffic and drive more efficiently, which increases the potential for less congestion on the roads.

The Internet of Things can also positively affect our education system by making it easier to collect data on students. For example, there could be sensors in schools that track how long a student has been on their computer or whether they've been paying attention. This could allow schools to see where students need more help and provide it to them.

The Internet of Things will also benefit our healthcare industry by making it easier for doctors and health professionals to analyze medical data. A doctor can use a medical device that reads your blood pressure, for example, as well as measure other physiological data from you. This will improve healthcare more than ever before because we'll be able to collect and analyze vast amounts of information in a relatively short period of time.

The Internet of Things will also improve our law enforcement by giving them more information on criminal activity and other threats that go on around the world into the future. Should we be concerned about this? Obviously, as a society, we have many concerns when it comes to privacy, safety, and security. However, I believe that keeping an eye on illegal activity going on around the world is important. It's important in order to help us protect ourselves against any possible dangers in our lives.

Index

A

Agile
 IoT product manager, 44–47
 product manager, 43
 society, 43
AI algorithms, 30, 31
Alphabet, 28, 29, 31
Amazon, 30, 176, 177
Amazon Web Services, 37, 38, 150
Analytics, 17, 53, 87, 149, 156
APIs, 38, 52, 74, 115
Apple, 30, 112, 176–178
Apple-owned Beats Electronics, 30
ApplesByte, 30
Application development, 118
Applications, 39, 85
Asana, 121, 128
Ashton, Kevin, 1–3, 151
Attributes, 69
Authority, 43, 54–56
Automation, 3, 28–33, 87, 176

B

Backend as a service (BaaS), 38
Banks, 82
Big data, 24
Big picture, 119

Bluetooth, 20, 34, 36, 47, 49, 82,
 141, 171, 173, 177
Bluetooth Low Energy (BLE), 47
BRITDOC Foundation Digital
 World conference, 2
Builders, 5
Building managers, 5, 7
Business model, 82, 114, 159
Business risks, 106–108
Business values, 48

C

Cambridge Silicon Radio
 (CSR), 42, 82
Canada Laws for IoT, 166–168
Capacity, 39, 74, 127, 132, 149
Career advice, 18
Career details, 17
Car sharing companies, 25
Cellular networks, 20
Cisco, 28
Cloud-based IoT, 105
Cloud-based platforms, 85, 87
Cloud-based services, 84
Cloud-based solutions, 45
Cloud-centric IOT
 platforms, 38, 39

Cloud computing, 99
   advanced skills, 54
   familiarity, 53
Cloud platforms, 34–37, 150
Coding, 49
Collaborative environment,
      122, 123
Comfort zones, 51
Commercialization, 92, 169
Communication, 5, 11, 17, 36, 39,
      75, 77, 84, 121, 150
Communication design, 99
Communication model, 87
Communication skills, 51
Communication technology, 20
Companies
   innovation in the space, 31–33
   IoT future, 29–31
   types, 28–34
Competencies, 76
Competition, 96, 137, 145, 169
Competitors, 28, 71, 95–97, 137,
      145, 146, 170, 178
Computer skills, 52
Computer systems, 88
Configurable sensors, 132
Connectivity, 8, 37, 38, 68, 75, 98,
      100, 104, 140, 161, 162, 164,
      165, 185
Consulting agencies, 50
Consumer, 8, 41, 99, 100, 140, 155
   demand, 42
Consumer-oriented
      applications, 88

Content delivery network, 38
Contractors, 5
Conventional devices, 102–104
Cooperative sensors, 132
Corporate social responsibility
      (CSR), 42
Costs, 17, 73, 97
Crisis, 71
Critical connections, 173, 174
Critical decisions, 136–139
Cross-functional teams, 69
Crowdfunding, 26, 82, 83
CSV file, 115
Customer experience, 24, 107
Customer management
      system, 94
Customer research, 11
Customers, 148
Customer satisfaction, 95
Customer service, 176
Cybersecurity, 162, 165

D

Dashboard, 63, 65, 115
Data analytics, 17, 67
Data collection, 32, 88, 133, 156
Data security, 170–173
Data selling, 156
Data visualization, 175
Department of Homeland Security
      (DHS), 165
Deploy, 92
Design and development, 91

Development stage, 90

Device management tools, 38

Device manufacturers, 158, 172

Devices, 1, 3, 20, 22, 35, 67, 85, 87, 98, 108, 118, 132, 152, 161, 163, 166, 171, 185

Device-to-cloud communication, 68

Device-to-device communication, 68

DevOps skills, 174

Digital education, 37

Digital health, 37

Digital products, 8

Digital strategy, 171

Distributed system, 173

Documentation, 15

Duties, 10–12

Dyson, Tony, 2

E

Edge-wise processing, 89

Education, 17, 37, 50, 60, 135, 167, 186

Electronic devices, 84, 87

Embedded development, 105

Employee
empowering, 56
experience, 56
morale, 56
turnover, 55

Employers, 6, 17, 45, 53

End-to-end development

competencies, 76

go-to-market strategy, 78, 79

quality assurance testing, 78, 79

responsibilities, 75

sales and marketing plan, 80

skills, 74

software development Teams, 76

End users, 11, 21, 41, 42, 56, 77–79, 93, 169

Energy consumption, 3, 5, 7

European Commission (EC), 162

European Union (EU), 161–163

Evaluation metrics, 94–97

Existing systems, 70

Expert, 160

F

Facebook, 84, 87

Factors, 12, 37, 52, 87, 96, 97, 103, 105, 119, 153

Failure, 57, 71, 96, 107

Federal Communications Commission (FCC), 163, 164, 168

Federal Trade Commission (FTC), 165

Filtering, 89

Finance, 27, 50

Firewall/security services, 38

First four months, 47–50

Five-step process, 21–23

Flexibility, 36, 37, 41, 164

G

GE Digital, 32
Geographical area, 87
Giant game changer, 4
Google, 26, 30, 31, 112, 178
Google Analytics, 67
Google Cloud IoT Platform, 37
Google-owned Nest, 29, 31–33
Go-to-market strategy, 78, 79
Government regulation
    Canada Laws for IoT, 166–168
    data security, 170–173
    EU, 161–163
    Internet, 161
    IoTPM, 174–176
    IoT products, 170–173, 176–178
    standards and
        regulations, 167–170
    US, 163–165
GPS devices, 154

H

Hackers, 152, 170, 171, 173
Hardware, 104–106, 132
    components, 33–37
    design, 84, 99, 101
    product management, 44
Hardware startups, 44
Healthcare, 3, 5, 50, 60, 117, 158, 167
Hewlett-Packard, 112
Home energy consumption
        activity, 88
HomeKit, 30

I, J

IBM, 26, 28, 30
IBM Bluemix, 37, 38
Ideal users, 21
Ideation, 90, 175
Industry 4.0, 26, 27
Information and
        communication, 24
Infrastructure as a service (IaaS), 38
Initial release, 85, 86
Innovation, 43, 140, 141, 163–165, 175
Integration, 90, 118
Intel, 1, 28, 31
Intelligence, 15, 112, 165, 175
Intelligent buildings, 7
Interconnection, 169
International Organization for
        Standardization (ISO), 168
International Telecommunication
        Union (ITU), 163
Internet, 2, 12, 20, 44, 60
Internet-controlled machines, 3
Internet infrastructure, 38
Internet of Medical Things
        (IoMT), 5
Internet of Things (IoT), 28, 44
    adoption, 5
    catalyst, 4
    cities, 4–7
    connectedness, 4
    convenience, 3
    description, 2
    duties and responsibilities, 10–12

employers, 6
functionality, 1
homes smart, 4–7
humans and machines, 4
innovation, 8
marketplace, 3
productivity and
    convenience, 1, 3
product manager, 8–10, 12–15
products and services, 7
sensors, 5
technologies, 4
workplaces, 6
Internet of Things manager
    (IoTM), 68,
    See also IoT Manager
Interoperability, 162–164
Investment crowdfunding, 82
Investments, 5, 21, 82, 83, 92, 104,
    106, 114, 167, 178
IoT business models, 23–25
    creation, 155
    new models, 159, 160
    revenue, 155
IoT data collection, 133
IoT data security, 170, 171
IoT development, 117–119
IoT device models, 54
IoT device monitoring, 132, 133
IoT devices, 83, 84, 86, 88
IoT gateway, 34, 143
IoT hardware components, 33–37
IoT implementation, 47
IoT landscape

Industry 4.0, 26, 27
physical objects, 25
IoT manager
    communication, 63
    dashboards, 65
    end-to-end development, 74–80
    IoT projects, 64
    IoT system, 64
    in organizations, 50–54
    questions, 66–68
    setting up, 65
    vendor or business partner, 64
IoT platforms, 35, 36, 84, 85
IoT product design, 92, 170–173
    applications, 36
    business models, 23–25
    communication technology, 20
    components, 20
    five-step process, 21–23
    hardware components, 33–37
    interconnectedness, 19
    programming platforms, 37–39
    real-world applications, 20
    technologies, 20
    three types of companies, 28–34
    user interface connection, 19
IoT product development
    business risks, 106–108
    companies, 98, 99
    considerations, 101, 102
    consumer, 99, 100
    conventional devices, 102–104
    drom scratch, 100, 101
    evaluation metrics, 94–97

IoT product development (*cont.*)
    hardware *vs.* software, 104–106
    life cycle, 90–94
    limited budget, 84
    market, 98
    seven steps, 81–87
    skills, 99
IoT product manager (IoTPM)
    authority, 54–56
    communicating with clients, 77
    competencies, 76
    critical condition, 136–139
    definition, 45
    device costs, 115
    first four months, 47–50
    four steps, security, 143, 144
    hardware product
        management, 44
    in-house research
        department, 112
    Internet, 44
    in organizations, 50–54
    IoT products, 176–178
    Iot *vs.* Software
        development, 117–119
    market, 113
    models and metrics, 112
    partners, 68–74
    practical steps, 45
    product metrics, 60–63
    quality assurance testing, 78, 79
    quantitative measurement
        structure, 60–63
    real product, 112
    research, 112–130
    responsibilities, 75
    skills, 174–177
    solutions to complex
        problems, 139–142
    stakeholders, 134–136
    team, 46, 47
    team management, 119–124
    technology vs. product, 46
    tips, 135
    valuable, 113
    visual dashboard, 115, 116
IoT product marketing, 146
    devices or products, 151
    IoT trends, 154–160
    key factors, 150
    quality IoT product, 150
    steps, 145–150
    strategy, 151–154
IoT products, 176–178
    sale, 154
IoT product strategy, 167–170
IoT prototype, 159
IoT road map, 58–60
IoT service, 21
IoT trends, 154–160
Iterative design process, 81

K

Key functionalities, 48
Key strategies, 172–174
Knowledge, 5, 8, 11, 13–15, 48, 52,
    53, 84, 106, 109, 118, 119

L

Learning, 14, 31, 33, 43, 46, 48, 63,
    139, 168, 169, 175
LED bulb, 17
Lenovo, 33
Licensing, 144
Life cycle, 13
    IoT product
        development, 90–94
    product, 92
Life cycle management, 135
Lifestyle choices, 6
LinkedIn, 87
Long-term strategy, 10

M

Machine to machine (M2M), 47
Maintenance, 93, 115, 117
Manufacturing, 3, 87, 101, 175, 186
Market, 41, 95, 113, 175
    size, 96
    target, 96
Marketing, 10, 11, 13, 15, 25, 26, 58,
        70, 78, 135, 147, 149,
        160, 178
Marketing plan, 80, 160
Marketing skills, 83
Marketing strategy, 151–154
Market opportunities, 81
Market research, 147
Mattermost, 121
McKinsey Global Institute, 7

McNally, James, 46
Metrics, 53, 62–65, 94–97
Microprocessor, 34
Microsoft, 26, 29
Microsoft Azure, 38
Microsoft Azure IoT, 37
Microsoft Excel, 74
Microsoft-owned Skype, 31, 32
Minimum viable product
        (MVP), 10
Mistakes, 106, 120, 142, 144, 183
Mobility, 24
Monetization, 156, 157
Multifamily, 60

N

National Institute of Standards and
        Technology (NIST), 168
Nest Hello, 33
Nest thermostat, 131
Network and device latency, 87
New products, 95
New product strategy, 70
NFC, 20
Nine phases, 90–93

O

Onboard, 49
Online platform, 86
On-premises systems, 87
Open Systems Interconnection
        (OSI) model, 168

Organisational skills, 54
Organizations, 50–54
Oversee operations, 11

P

Paraphrasing, 46
People management, 46
Percentage stake, 82
Performance-driven growth, 68–74
Personalized advertising, 24
Personnel and training, 73
Physical interface, 162
Piwik, 67
Platform as a service (PaaS), 38
Product acceptance, 95
Product adoption, 68–74
Product backlog management
    configurable sensors, 132
    cooperative sensors, 132
    features, 131–133
    IoT business strategy, 130
    limited functionality, 130
    nest thermostat, 131
    prioritization, 133, 134
    sensors, 131
Product features, 132
Product interface, 94
Productivity, 3, 24
Product life cycle management
    (PLM), 175
Product management, 17, 18, 174
    activities and skills, 109
    manager, 109

roles, 140, 141
in software, 109
students, 109
tips, 110
Product managers, 8–10, 74
    agile, 43
    business and
        technologies, 13–15
    career advice, 18
    career description, 17, 18
    career details, 17
    digital world, 12
    product definition, 13
    product team, 12
    reasons, hired, 16–19
    skills, 14
    specialists, 15
    value chain, 14
Product metrics, 60–63
Product ownership, 175
Product road map, 49
    steps, 58–60
    strategic plan, 57
    user-centric product, 57
Product strategic
        decisions, 124–126
Profit, 6, 8, 37, 56, 94, 97, 160
Profitability, 138
Programming platforms, 37–39
Progress report, 71
Project goals, 72
Project management, 52
Project tasks, 72
Provisioning, 38, 92, 176

Q

QlikView, 67
Qualifications, 17
Quality, 5, 7, 56, 138, 148–150,
      168, 169
Quality assurance testing, 78, 79
Quantitative measurement
      structure, 60–63

R

Real-time interaction, 20
Recognition, 56
Replication, 89
Resilience, 165
Responsibilities, 10–12
RESTful Web Services, 52
Revenue, 11, 95, 154–160
Risks, 25, 61, 97, 106–108, 134,
      135, 168
Road map, 49

S

Salaries, 17, 18
Sales, 11, 13, 15, 70, 80, 93–96, 112,
      115, 116, 135, 148, 159, 165
Samsung, 29, 32
Satellite networks, 20
Scaling, 92, 146
Science fiction, 152
Scratch, 10, 47, 101, 102, 118
Scrum, 134
Security, 39, 94, 141, 158, 169

Security and safety, 7
Self-created project, 48
Sensor-equipped item, 2
Sensors, 8, 33, 34, 52, 87, 131
Server latency, 88
Servers, 38, 74, 87, 88, 177
Short-term revenue targets, 11
Skills, 74, 174–177
Skill set, 84
Small startups, 82
Smart home tech company, 29
Smartphone, 24, 178
Smartphone cameras, 177
Social media, 87
Software, 104–106, 132
Software as a service (SaaS), 38
Software components, 87
Software development, 99,
      115, 117–119
Software development life cycle
      (SDLC), 54, 123
Software development
      programmer, 13
Software development teams, 76
Software product managers, 18
Software startups, 44
Solutions to complex
      problems, 139–142
Sony, 29
Sony-owned Sony Smart Audio
      Technology, 31
SQL Server Management
      Studio, 74
Stabilization, 3

Stakeholders, 11, 68–74, 134–136, 138

Standard interfaces, 22

Startup approach, 174

Straightforward working style, 123

Strategic decision making, 125

Strategies, 69, 89, 90

Streaming, 89

Streamlining, 55

Subtasks, 120

Success, 96

Systems development, 118

T

Tableau, 67

Tactical decision, 126, 127

Tasks, 122

Team, 10, 11, 13, 16, 46, 47, 64, 65, 69, 103, 108, 121, 141, 142

Team management, 49
    collaborative environment, 122, 123
    communication, 121
    product strategic decisions, 124–126
    project manager, 119
    subtasks, 120
    tactical decision, 126, 127
    timelines, 120
    time management structures, 127–131

    tools, 121, 122

Team player, 53

Team's strengths, 137

Technology, 7, 13, 28, 32, 46–48, 109, 111, 113, 117, 151, 167, 168

Testers, 11, 62, 93

Time allocation, 70

Time management structures, 127–131

Tracks data, 86

Transportation, 3

Transportation sector, 3

Trello, 121

Trends, 157–159

Trust, 122

Twitter, 87

U

Unique value propositions, 145

United States (US), 163–165

Universal service, 169

User-centric product, 57

User experience design, 21

User feedback, 10

User interface, 19, 22

User research, 137

Users, 95

V

Value chain, 14

Venture capitalists (VC), 82

Verbal communications, 16

Vision for the product, 72
Visualization, 133
Vivint, 29
Voice-activated learning, 33

W

Website, 58, 79, 80, 83, 84, 93,
 103, 160
Wi-Fi, 34, 36, 47, 87, 171, 173

Win-win partnership, 82
Wireless networks, 34

X, Y

Xiaomi, 32

Z

Zehner, Jacki, 2
Zigbee, 34, 36, 47, 49, 119

Printed in the United States
by Baker & Taylor Publisher Services